Good Things Happen
in Glasgow

Good Things Happen in Glasgow

Jude Addo

To order additional copies of this book, contact:
Xlibris LLC
0-800-056-3182
www.xlibrispublishing.co.uk
Orders@xlibrispublishing.co.uk
635864

CONTENTS

Foreword

Preamble – Precursor – Preview

I never imagined that a day would come when I would be asked to write anything worth publishing. In fact, I was a bit sceptical when Jude asked me to write this foreword as I am so far from being or becoming an author. I clearly remember the day Jude got the inspiration for this book and the title after a speaking engagement at a youth conference in London. We laughed at the idea, but he wrote down the title anyway, just in case.

Well, 'just in case' turned out to be a pipe dream, but one that has materialized into what you now hold in your hands. This dream is as personal to Jude as it is to me. Good Things Happen in Glasgow or GTHIG (gee-thig) tells a unique story of love in various dimensions. Jude shares the trials and temptations, perseverance and patience that both he and I have endured during the course of our relationship, right from our very first meeting in Glasgow (surprise!) to our engagement and life post-engagement.

To say our relationship has been a smooth journey would be telling a lie. We have had our fair share of bumpy rides and ups and downs which have only made our love and commitment for one another deeper and stronger. I do not think I have ever prayed about any situation in my life as much as I have about our relationship. This union is a testimony in and of itself. Regardless of whatever situation you may find yourself in, 'many are the plans in a man's heart, but it is the LORD's purpose that prevails' (Prov 19:21).

The above-mentioned verse does not mean it will be easy or that there will not be setbacks. There will be times where you get hurt and feel like giving up. As long as it is the will of God, submit your plans totally and wholeheartedly, trusting in Him completely and it will be made perfect in your life.

I now leave you with the words of Jude. I pray that GTHIG blesses you and that the words of this book inspire and encourage you. Indeed, good things do happen in Glasgow!

Olamide A.

To the couple who I can't thank enough for
their love, support, and direction—
Rt. Rev. Dick Essandoh and his wife, Lady Agnes Essandoh

Prologue

Preface – Purpose – Plot

Terrific—I allowed myself to get talked into writing another book. I simply cannot express just how delighted I am to write my second paperback after record sales of my debut book, *Crossroads*. I'm essentially a millionaire now—not.

Excusing the levity, I am immensely grateful to God for the numerous testimonies I have received from those blessed by reading *Crossroads*. It is rather gratifying to know that what appeared to be an attempt at book writing in a medium-sized apartment in East London transformed the lives of several people across varied geographies.

Although I may never become a *New York Times* bestselling author, which you can be assured is no goal of mine, I am constantly reminded that I have been called to play the background and Christ takes centre stage, no matter how big or small that stage is. A call is a call, and in view of this philosophy I have chosen unreservedly to answer mine which, strangely, has led to this new book entitled *Good Things Happen in Glasgow*. Now, I know what you're probably thinking after reading that title, *Great, he's getting soft on us with a rom-com book*. Let me take a moment to declare the contrary. I neither have plans to enter the chick-flick industry now nor in the near future. The thought alone of seeing my name printed on the cover of a book with the aforementioned title made my carnal nature cringe.

Perhaps this is due to the foolish depiction of masculinity society has so imbibed in us. Or perchance my own foolishness in thinking my street cred would be compromised. Oh, you didn't know? I've got street cred—not. I do concede, however, that aspects of this book speak to certain biblical themes using several experiences during my period of courtship as a backdrop. Therefore, it was a near impossible task to avoid romanticizing the description of events mentioned throughout the pages of this novel.

The thought alone of seeing my name printed on the cover of a book with the aforementioned title made my carnal nature cringe.

As you can imagine, this was a tough book to write for one who grew up religiously devoted to the preaching of Tupac and the church of gangster rap. Family was the gang, the hood was home, government was evil, and rebellion was masculinity at its finest. The former amateur gangster rapper who ate bullets for lunch (yes, those were one of my lyrics) now writes books about God and love—if that isn't miraculous then I have not a clue about the supernatural. Indeed, what you hold in your hands is an outward manifestation of an inner swallowing of pride and abdication of machismo in the hope that somehow, someone will come to the knowledge of the saving grace of Jesus.

So why the unorthodox title for a book centrally themed on Christian values? Well, I thought it was catchy. And a bit corny. But I took a chance on it anyway—sue me. Be convinced nevertheless that there is a subliminal message behind the title which will by all means be made apparent during the course of this book.

I regularly get asked by *Crossroads* enthusiasts when the next book is expected to be released. To that, I always candidly respond with 'we shall see', with the view that the line of questioning would end there. With my kind of luck, it never does. At the behest of these wonderful people, here goes nothing. Be mindful though that I have not decided to fabricate a load of chaff in response to popular demand. God has placed a message in my heart and the enthusiasm of readers has been the much needed encouragement to translate that message into my second volume.

In this message, I highlight various observations I have made about the state of the Church, the mindset of believers, and the growing plight of religious division across the globe using Africa, the cradle of civilization, as the focal talking point. Of course, many other themes will emerge and be discussed, including rejection, forgiveness, and love, drawing upon a variety of biblical references. During this journey, we will pay respect to the Queen in London, get a tan in the heat of Accra, and experience some power outages on the streets of Abuja. Oh, and we just might take a detour for some haggis in Glasgow—if that's your kind of thing.

But do good things *really* happen in Glasgow? I guess we'll just have to wait and see.

One

Hitbodedut

Separation – Seclusion – Supplication

On any other day, I'd be getting off the Jubilee line at Canning Town after a long day in the city reporting profit and loss breaks to the business heads of the Equity Derivatives Group. The only thing I would look forward to at that moment was the imminent pacifying conversation with my other half that promised to take my mind off the workload and the fact that there really was nothing to eat at home—it's a hard knock life for a bachelor I tell you. Except, this time, things were different.

I was now taking the train from the Wharf, analysing market risk for the Rates business, and was certainly not expecting any phone call as I disembarked the train at Canning Town. The one thing that hadn't changed was the food situation—there was still none to come home to.

It was a struggle coming to terms with single life. The lady I had just shared the past six years of my youth with was no longer in the picture. Frankly, I wasn't so sure that even I was in the picture, or what the picture was meant to look like. I had spent such a large portion of my adolescence in relationships that I couldn't be certain I was my own person at the point of separation. Albeit necessary, this separation was exceedingly difficult to deal with. The apartment had an empty feel to it, my mobile phone seemed to never ring, and I saw myself increasingly creeping into a shell of solitude.

Whenever my phone rang, it was probably a Saturday. And yes, it was probably Mum.

'Papa, how are you doing?'

'Grace abounds, Ma', I would always say in a cheerful tone to avoid her getting worried.

'Great', she would often reply, telling me how tough the economy in Ghana was but reassuring me that God was providing as usual. She would then ask, 'So, have you eaten, Papa, did you cook?'

To which I would reply, 'No, God hasn't provided a chef yet, but I'm keeping the faith.'

Not at all. I never said that. But I was thinking it. I perceive that she was inquisitive about my eating habits primarily because she wanted to know whose food I was consuming—you know how iffy African mothers can get about things like that and with just cause, of course.

It was almost as if I had grown up treating affection as a drug and now that it was no longer there, I was experiencing withdrawal symptoms. There was no one to call me 'baby' or any other terms of endearment that I had become so accustomed to since the age of sixteen. In hindsight, I think that was a tad young to be engaged in non-platonic relationships. In any case, to get through this period I would often invite one of my mentees, William, for sleepovers involving banter, FIFA, food, and when we got around to it, a little prayer. This arrangement kept me level-headed and certainly safeguarded me from the charming guise of mischief. Irrespective of how spiritual or sanctified one is, practical steps should always be employed when dealing with the issues that life throws at us—just my two cents.

So I carried on like this for weeks, maybe months. This was until I developed a rather distinct conviction that the companionship I was keeping was a cheap substitute for the relationship I was actually meant to be improving during my period of solitude—that between myself and God.

Hitbodedut.

There is no point getting the dictionary—I'll help you out. Hitbodedut (pronunciation: *hisbodedus*—don't ask) refers to a Jewish practice where one secludes himself in order to spend some time in prayer and meditation. The aim is to gain a clearer understanding of one's personal motives and aspirations. I'll be the first to admit that this form of devotion was not my initial intention although I did see the need to spend more time soul searching.

For about three months, I began to draw very close to God, so close that it felt like I was on cloud nine. You know that feeling, when you deem within yourself that you haven't consciously sinned in thought, deed, word or motive for a sustained period and you begin to pat yourself on the back for it . . . No? It's just me? Well, I guess I'm in need of more help than I thought. This was the time in which I began to question God, not out of doubt, but out of a sincere longing to understand exactly what He was up to in my life. Why did this relationship have to last six years just to come to an end? Was it even worth it? Why did I have to go through all of that for something that wouldn't last? And of course, I couldn't help calculating all the money I had spent during the course of that relationship on gifts and trips, wondering how financially sound I could have been if I had instead placed those funds in an interest bearing time deposit. Yes, I know I'm a tad special.

What subsequently became my resolve was most likely a product of my frustration. I decided to stay single for the next few years and maybe consider marriage at some point in my mid-thirties . . . to a Ghanaian. How narrow-minded, right? I share the same view. But at that point, I couldn't bring myself to go against the grain. In a moment, I'll explain what I mean.

Up until this time, I had been dating a Nigerian. This relationship had been active since our high school days and had survived the tribulations of the distance between London and Rhode Island where she and I attended university respectively. Both our parents had treated the relationship with flippancy until the tenure thereof became somewhat of an indication of the prospective next step . . . you guessed it—the M word. A plethora of questions followed with one inquiry underpinning them all: are you absolutely sure you can marry a Nigerian? The converse of that question was posed to her as well, obviously. Now, undeniably these questions came from a good place— it goes without saying that each of our families had become incredibly fond of us. However, they simply wanted to make sure that we knew what we were signing up for as, contrary to popular belief, it *is* a lifetime commitment. To my dismay, the frenzied deliberation continued until the families had gained absolute comfort that we had full consciousness of what we were getting ourselves into, being prepared in advance for potential issues of contention in marriage.

I decided to stay single for the next few years and maybe consider marriage at some point in my mid-thirties . . . to a Ghanaian.

Now, that relationship was over. There was no way I ever planned to go through the pain of that debate again—ever. You may appreciate why I became excessively adamant against non-Ghanaian relationships. Apart from the fact that I had completely no appetite for that sort of pressure again, I also came to the realisation that ever since I began to notice the opposite sex, I had not really taken a serious interest in authentic Ghanaian ladies. As strange as that may have been, pursuing a Ghanaian woman sometime in the future became sort of an adventure for me, and one that I was keenly looking forward to.

I tried to take these plans to God in prayer:

'Father, let your will be done—but please, no more Nigerians. Amen.'

That petition somehow crept its way into my prayers whenever I communed with God. But God had other plans, apparently.

• • •

May 14th. The day I'm officially obliged to remember. I found myself in the south of Scotland on a short business trip to work alongside our Scottish counterparts on a technology project. I knew not a single soul in this part of the world, except for the fact that an older brother of a friend lived and studied somewhere in Glasgow. To escape boredom and simultaneously strengthen my network, I arranged dinner with him for 7 p.m. True to African timeliness, he showed up at 8 p.m., with his girlfriend . . . and another friend. I had heard of a plus one, but plus two? I didn't know that was the in thing; I must have missed the memo.

As we boarded the taxi to the restaurant, I welcomed my friend along with his better half whom I had coincidentally known on a personal basis for several years during high school. It was great to see their faces again. I then courteously introduced myself to their plus one, realizing that I had neither rendered her the due notice nor attention. In all honesty, I was not interested in making new friends at the time (hashtag, no new friends) and certainly not those of the opposite sex. It was my inner purpose to remain in solitude and focus on myself. However, after noticing her charming smile, I couldn't help but momentarily toy with the idea that she could be a potential candidate—that was until I asked for her name.

'I'm Jude. It's a pleasure to meet you, what's your name?' I asked, reaching out my hand for a firm, formal handshake.

'Nice to meet you too. My name is Olamide,' She amiably responded, reciprocating the grip.

'I'm sorry, what was your name again?' I asked the second time, genuinely requesting clarification as it was not a name I had come across until then. And yes, it sounded like a Nigerian name too.

She confirmed it. She was Nigerian. Every idea concerning a possible future that I had temporarily entertained immediately came to a halt. Forget it—it's not happening.

I tried to take these plans to God in prayer: 'Father, let your will be done—but please, no more Nigerians. Amen.'

As you can imagine, the rest of the evening dining at Horton's was slightly uncomfortable for me, making every effort to remain cordial to this lovely lady yet maintaining a strong sense of emotional distance to avoid building a meaningful relationship. It didn't work—by the end of the evening we had shared a meal, laughs, and unforgettable memories. Lord, have mercy.

After weeks of talking and getting to know each other a bit better, we mutually decided to give this thing a shot by praying together and building a stronger friendship. Well, I put up a front as if it was mutual. I was still very apprehensive about getting involved in anything that would remotely resemble a relationship, especially after only six months of dissolving a six-year relationship with another non-Ghanaian lady.

Boy was I confused, so mentally burdened that I had to set up a meeting with my mentor.

'Bish, we've got to talk, please.'

'What's it about, son?'

'Well, there's this lady . . .'

'The women are troubling you, eh?' He interjects.

'Not at all,' I respond, chuckling with embarrassment. 'I met this lady in Glasgow—we're talking, and I really like her . . .

but, as you know I just came out of a long-term relationship, and this lady is not Ghanaian.'

During the course of our lengthy conversation, he said a few words that intensified my appreciation for the wisdom he carries. I left his office with the understanding that even if it was God's will for Olamide and I to be together, which would be revealed in God's own time, we had to ensure that we adequately prepared ourselves in advance for issues arising from the disparities, albeit few, in culture. So that's what we did. We spent the summer months devoted to fasting, praying, and educating ourselves on each other's culture through conversation—and Wikipedia. This was until the uncertainty as to what the future held led me to pray some rather daring prayers. I was at a point where I knew the clatter in my mind would not permit me to hear the voice of God. So this became my plea:

'Lord, if you're speaking concerning this relationship then I am certain I cannot hear You, so please send someone to come and tell me what you're saying.'

The rest of the story is hard to believe, but were it not for the fact that there were scores of people to bear witness, I would probably be hesitant to narrate it. A few weeks later, I had literally touched down in London from Glasgow on a similar trip for work when I received a text message from a friend reminding me of a Friday church service with a visiting minister that night. Frankly, I couldn't be bothered to make it, and I had already made plans to visit the lady friend. As understanding as she is, she agreed to cancel our evening plans and attend the church service with me. What a decision that turned out to be.

This visiting minister, whom neither of us had ever met or heard of before, carried a prophetic gift and he spent most of the service prophesying to the congregation and leading specific prayer topics for certain people. Two hours into the service, he began conspicuously searching the pews as if being led to a specific person. At this point, I was getting nervous, hoping to God he didn't call me out. He looked in my direction for a moment, pointed his finger (I almost died), and called out my guest who was seated beside me. In relief, I whispered praises to God for hearing my prayers. With my kind of luck, this adulation did not last even one minute. The visiting minister came back, called me out this time and kindly asked me to stand next to her. Lord, have mercy.

The pastor asked if we knew each other, further enquiring as to whether we were friends or siblings. We then stood by our story and insisted we were just friends, knowing very well that was not the complete truth—he wasn't buying it either. In a brief moment, I will share with you the words he spoke to us, directly confirming our prayers for God's will to be revealed. These were his words, in summary: 'There is a prophetic connection between the two of you; do not let each other go for the union has a great purpose'. Boom. He had just dropped a bomb on us.

'Lord, if you're speaking concerning this relationship then I am certain I cannot hear You, so please send someone to come and tell me what you're saying.'

This wasn't quite how I expected things to pan out in my life. I had originally planned to be single and pursue a Ghanaian woman sometime in the distant future. Now here I was, madly in love with a Nigerian and having confirmation that she was the one. For comfort, I had to tally this experience with scripture and boy, did God help me do just that.

Two

Eden

Creation – Calling – Communion

I had to come to an understanding of why God would completely knock me out of my period of solitary devotion and present a woman to me for the long haul, particularly at a time when I was neither looking nor interested. This baffled me for months, until I was led to the book of Genesis—the beginning—the first union that occurred between man and woman under the sanction of God.

Allow me to forewarn you that what you are about to read may challenge your theological predisposition. The revelation I received concerning the creation of man is rather unconventional and expands on what I learnt at Sunday school. All the same, I believe it represents a new dimension of understanding that could only empower the Church.

I want to start by looking at creation. By reason of our upbringing, most people of Christian faith would affirm with hand on heart that Adam and Eve were the first created human beings. However, very few truly appreciate the purpose for which God created them. From the very first verse in Genesis, we see God's creative handiwork in crafting a distinction between land and sea, day and night, and plant and animal. At the climax of it all, he creates man—both male and female—and grants them dominion over all living things:

Then God said, 'Let Us make man in Our image, according to Our likeness; and let them rule over the fish of the sea and over the birds of the sky and over the cattle and over all the earth, and over every creeping thing that creeps on the earth.' God *created man* in His own image, in the image of God He created him; male and female He created them. God blessed them; and God said to them, '*Be fruitful and multiply*, and fill the earth . . .' (*Gen 1:26–28*).

It may surprise you to learn that the creation of Adam was instigated by a specific purpose, a calling, a ministry. This truth is only revealed in the second chapter of Genesis:

Now no shrub of the field was yet in the earth, and no plant of the field had yet sprouted, for the LORD God had not sent rain upon the earth, and *there was no man to cultivate* the ground. The LORD God planted a garden toward the east, in Eden; and *there He placed the man* whom He had formed (*Gen 2:5, 8*).

By reason of our upbringing, most people of Christian faith would affirm with hand on heart that Adam and Eve were the first created human beings. However, few understand the purpose for which God created them.

God created a unique being purposely for a special ground. The ground for which God needed cultivation was that of Eden, which in Hebraic literature means 'bliss' or 'delight' and is synonymous with 'paradise'. From the study of the scriptures, we understand paradise as the dwelling place of God, where God's presence is experienced by mankind. It is the place where man meets God. See where I'm going with this? No? All right, I'll spell it out. Adam was purposely created to live and work in the presence of God, as a minister of God, doing the work of God by cultivating the ground. Yes, Adam was the first high priest during the dispensation of creation; the only one allowed to enter the holy of holies—Eden—and commune with God in the cool of the day (see *Gen 3:8*).

Adam was no ordinary man. He was fashioned primarily to be the chief priest who dwelt in the presence of God—in constant Hitbodedut. This was his calling. For this reason, mankind fell when Adam fell. It wasn't solely because Adam was the first born of creation, which strictly speaking is actually Jesus Christ (see *Col 1:14-15*). Mankind fell because the one who was given the remit to be in the presence of God constantly making intercession for the rest of humanity had himself fallen. If the chief priest is no longer sanctified, how can those under him for whom he makes intercession be sanctified? It follows the same principle as 'strike the shepherd and the sheep will scatter'.

● ● ●

Adam, a minister of God in isolated communion with The Father, dwelt in a place God had prepared for cultivation called Eden. With that understanding, let's examine what happens next:

Then the LORD God said, 'It is not good for *the* man to be alone; I will make him a helper *suitable* for him' (*Gen 2:18*).

Boom. God dropped a bomb on Adam. Allow me to highlight a few things that are very interesting about this verse.

First of all, Adam was not actually alone. This was paradise, the presence of God could be felt daily. God himself was dwelling with Adam in Eden, Adam was in the presence of The Father in the original holy of holies. But God still said it was not good for him to be alone. This is the first indication of the importance God places on companionship in ministry.

Secondly, we often quote this verse missing the definite article 'the'. God said it was not good for *the* man to be alone— not just any man, but this specific man, Adam. Why is that? This is simply because Adam was a man in ministry; a man who had been called by God for a specific purpose. And this is why God's solution was to create a helper who would be *suitable* to that purpose—a woman who would help him achieve the calling that God had intended for him. I know, it's rather ironic how things turned out to be the exact opposite, right? But I believe that God had a plan all along.

Thirdly, isn't it interesting how God did all of this without consulting Adam? In essence, God looked at Adam and thought to Himself, *this isn't working,* and decided to marry him off for the sake of the ministry. No questions asked. The most intriguing thing here is this: God decided to put Adam into a deep sleep, knowing very well that if Adam was fully alert he would have objected to the marriage. I'll tell you why. Adam was in a place of bliss—what more did he need? The man had no lack. God had already provided everything He needed. Or so he thought. And the autonomy of doing what he wanted, when he wanted, and not having to take another's feelings into consideration must have seemed very appealing.

Adam woke up one day and all of a sudden there was a lady in his life—from nowhere. He had neither requested a wife, nor had he pursued one. He had been enjoying his period of Hitbodedut. Yet somehow, he knew this union was of God, divinely inspired, orchestrated, and sanctioned.

So the LORD God caused *a deep sleep* to fall upon the man, and he slept; then He took one of his ribs and closed up the flesh at that place. The LORD God fashioned into a woman the rib which He had taken from the man, and *brought her to the man*. The man said, 'This is now bone of my bones, and flesh of my flesh . . .' (*Gen 2:21-23*).

The realisation that my experience was in tandem with the scriptures gave me comfort, being assured that truly God had a plan. Like Adam, I was thoroughly enjoying my period of isolation and communion with God and out of the blue, a lady suddenly appeared in my life uninvited. But one who was brought in to help with the ministry and calling God had purposed.

Adam woke up one day and all of a sudden there was a lady in his life—from nowhere.

It would intrigue you to know that the experience of Adam and Eve in the Old Testament is mirrored by Christ in the New Testament. The Bible begins and ends with a marriage; it begins with the marriage between Adam and Eve, and ends with the marriage between Christ and the Church—coincidence? I think not. I'd like to draw a few parallels here.

The first observation has to do with Hitbodedut. Before Adam was given Eve as his wife, he went through a period of seclusion and isolated communion with God. In the same way, the Gospels record how Christ would habitually leave his disciples and isolate himself to pray and commune with God. This was before Jesus died—akin to falling into a *deep sleep*—rose again, and took the Church as His Bride.

But Jesus often withdrew to *lonely places and prayed* (*Luke 5:15*).

In addition, you would notice that Eve was fashioned from the rib of Adam. This was the reason he called her 'flesh of my flesh'. The Bible goes on to say this in Genesis:

For this reason a man shall leave his father and his mother, and be joined to his wife; and they *shall become one flesh* (*Gen 2:24*).

The concept of being one through the agency of marriage is replicated by the bond Christ has with the Church. The New Testament declares that believers in Jesus are now one with Christ, who is also one with God.

I have been crucified with Christ; and it is no longer I who live, but Christ lives in me (*Gal 2:20*).

To avoid monopolizing this point, I'll end with a final parallel. Christ, our new High Priest in the dispensation of redemption, came to replace the original high priest in the dispensation of creation—Adam.

Therefore, just as through one man sin entered into the world, and death through sin, and so death spread to all men, because all sinned. Nevertheless death reigned from Adam until

Moses, even over those who had not sinned in the likeness of the offense of Adam, *who is a type of Him who was to come (Rom 5:12, 14)*.

This passage of scripture further validates the fact that Adam was the first high priest known to mankind. For this reason, Christ was tested not in His capacity as the Son of God, but as the divinely appointed High Priest of mankind in order to overthrow the curse introduced through the fall of Adam in Genesis. The verse above reinforces the significance of Christ's ministry—the one Adam was unable to fulfil. Christ redeemed both mankind and the priesthood, for where Adam caused humanity to fall by the priesthood, Christ restored humanity via the same means:

For we do not have a *high priest* who is unable to empathize with our weaknesses, but we have one who has been tempted in every way, just as we are—*yet he did not sin (Heb 4:15)*.

• • •

This chapter is not aimed at painting the picture that this is the only way God sanctions marriage, that would be putting God in a box and would be outright false. It would not be the case in all instances that a man or woman would just show up in your life. God isn't a one-trick pony. If you take a look at the life of Isaac for example, a messenger was sent to find him a suitable wife, Rebecca. Also, Jacob had to settle for Leah for an initial seven years before pursuing the woman he truly loved, Rachel, for another seven years. There are dynamics to dealing with God especially with regards to the union of a man and a woman.

However, there are a few things we can glean from the events that transpired in the Garden. The first is simple: as a man in ministry, it is not good for you to be alone. One man cannot achieve the call of God on his life by himself—it is usually too big. A helper is needed:

Two are better than one because they have a good return for their labour (*Eccles 4:9*).

Secondly, as a bride it is ideal to look for a man who dwells in the presence of God. Note that Eve was given a man who was constantly in a place called Eden—the dwelling place of The Lord. In the same vein, the Church is the bride of Jesus Christ—the one and only Son of God who is in constant communion with The Father. This is the sort of attribute you should look for in a man (or woman). Prayer is key when it comes to life and relationships—a day without prayer is a boast against God. It will do you some good if your partner is prayerful.

Finally, remember to accept whatever the will of God is—God knows best. Adam had no plans to be joined to a woman in marriage but he accepted the will of God. Jesus actually preferred not to go to the cross which implies that He wouldn't have been given the Church as a bride, yet He went ahead with the will of God all the same:

Saying, 'Father, if You are willing, remove this cup from Me; yet not My will, but Yours be done' (*Luke 22:42*).

This also helps us appreciate the fact that God sometimes gives you gifts that you have never prayed for. And often times, those are the best gifts—they originate from genuine thoughts for you that exceed anything you could have ever imagined for yourself:

For I know the thoughts that I think toward you, saith the LORD, thoughts of peace, and not of evil, to give you an expected end (*Jer 29:11*).

A day without prayer is a boast against God. It will do you some good if your partner is prayerful.

Similar to Adam's experience in the Garden, I had no plans of getting married, let alone to a lady who isn't Ghanaian. I had not asked God for female company; neither was I praying for a wife. But I had to accept the will of God for what it was, knowing that His plans would turn out to be much better than mine. And so far, I haven't been proved wrong.

Three

The Ring

Trouble – Trial – Temptation

I once heard a wise man say, 'There are three rings when it comes to marriage—the telephone ring, the engagement ring, and then the boxing ring'. Experientially speaking, truer words have never been spoken.

Following the prophetic revelation, our relationship continued to strengthen daily, building on the foundation of a healthy friendship. It's probably worth noting that physical attraction increased exponentially too—for some reason, I guess that I initially hadn't realized how beautiful she was. Or maybe she was just putting in more effort this time around—who knows. It's probably safe to say that this was our 'honeymoon period'—things were good, and incredibly so.

Clearly, this was the telephone ring stage.

We would literally spend hours on phone calls with no break, which was rather surprising to me as one who naturally disliked telephone conversations. If I was cooking, she would know—in fact, she would see what was on the cooker and have an input in what I was making. We went to bed at night hearing each other's voice and woke up hearing each other's voice. Not a day went by without having an extensive conversation. We thank the good Lord for the lives of Janus Friis and Niklas Zennström—founders of Skype.

Following several months of courtship, I finally decided to ask for Olamide's hand in marriage, which must have been the most difficult decision I have made to date. As a man, I was naturally averse to locking myself down for life. Worse still, as one who was only twenty-four years old, the thought that I could be making a mistake almost chocked me to death. Additionally, I knew some of my peers would have thought that I had probably lost some bolts up there, but I had never been one to falter at the words of antagonists. It took weeks of prayer and meditation to finally come to the point where I was comfortable enough to utter those words. Either that or I had to be drunk or high, neither of which was an option for a man in my position. So I prayed, and prayed, and prayed, and prayed some more.

'God, are you sure I should go ahead with this?'

The conviction was strong, but I still couldn't bring myself to take that leap of faith. As a result, I recruited one of her friends, Ama, to help me find a ring. Guys, a little piece of advice here—this is simultaneously the best and worst decision you could ever make. Your special lady will certainly get the ring she wants, but definitely at the price you don't. All the same, this was a major step in becoming obedient to what I felt God was asking me to do.

As a man, I was naturally averse to locking myself down for life. Worse still, as one who was only twenty-four years old, the thought that I could be making a mistake almost chocked me to death.

The events that followed confirmed my conviction. At the jewellery store, Ama and I communally agreed on a ring but we weren't quite sure what size Olamide was. After paying for the precious stone, we walked out of the high-street store with excitement, knowing that we had selected the perfect ring. However, half way to the tube station, I developed a strong sense of buyer's remorse with respect to the ring size we had chosen. I had no idea what size she was, but I felt deeply within myself that she couldn't have been the size we settled on.

The jeweller proposed that I ask her to marry me with the ring I had bought and return it for the correct size in the unlikely event that the ring did not fit. My ego would never allow me to do such a thing—if I was going to do it I had to get it right. I took a chance and went two sizes down. With the benefit of hindsight, I am convinced it was God's guidance from the outset. But here's the thing, that particular store in Central London did not have the smaller ring size; the closest store was over an hour's train ride outside London. Quite frankly, it was a discouraging journey but I was a man on a mission. I couldn't allow an incorrect ring size to rob me of my swagger. Going through all that trouble, I couldn't help but think to myself, *This woman better like this ring, or else . . .*

And she did. She loved it!

I remember asking her to marry me. I sat her down and took a seat beside her, bringing out the bling. She was speechless.

'Oh my God, Oh my God, Oh my God,' she repeatedly muffled in panic.

'Am I going to get an answer?' I recurrently asked. I knew she was going to say yes (I think), but she stalled for so long that I was beginning to question my chances.

'Oh my God, Oh my God, Oh my God,' she carried on. Then after what felt like the longest minute I had ever experienced, she gestured with her eyes pointing down to the floor. That's right—she was expecting me to get down on one knee before she gave me an answer.

See what you've done to our women, Hollywood? You should be ashamed.

To make a point, I went down on my left knee. Those close to me understand the significance of that gesture. It was the knee that had undergone keyhole surgery a few months prior.

She said yes. I slipped on the ring. Perfect fit.

And I felt like a million dollars. After the money I had spent on that rock it was quite surprising that I felt like anything above overdraft. The bank account was slightly bruised but boy was it worth it. I was an engaged man.

I vividly recall this proposal being the subject of wide-ranging reactions from both sides of the spectrum: 'Atta boy!' from my siblings to 'I'm so happy for you' from my female friends. 'What did she say?' from my parents to 'Ey, Jude, are you sure?' from one of my close pals. Some had convinced themselves that I was rushing into marriage whilst others believed it was a ploy to expedite sexual intimacy. The variance was endless. The reaction that beat them all was that of my own inner conscience—'well done for obedience'. I was at peace with the decision and, for me, that was the most important thing.

• • •

A few weeks into the engagement things began to feel a bit different. It no longer felt like the honeymoon period anymore. Well, certainly not for me. Arguments were persistent and difficult to resolve, temptation was around me more often than welcome, sickness became an imminent threat to life and happiness, workload from both work and ministry appeared to have quadrupled, and the sudden change in my spending patterns was almost crippling. According to the self-fulfilling prophecy, I had now found myself in the boxing ring—the fight was on.

I often wondered, 'God, if this is your will why on earth am I experiencing so many unnecessary problems? Am I being punished for something here? Did I get this wrong?' This episode undeniably played games with my psyche, questioning whether or not the proposal was the right move to make at that point in time.

It was hectic. The calendar was full to the brim. I didn't even have time for myself and you know when that happens, by implication you surely do not have time for God. I was working late nights, serving in church three to four days a week, constantly attending to the needs of the youth that I mentored, organizing an annual youth conference in Ghana, and of course, I had to make time for the lady. No pressure—piece of cake.

Not really. I struggled—big time.

I knew I had arrived at the point of inflection when I began entertaining the idea of scaling down my time commitment to the local church and I had developed a pretty convincing argument for doing so too. I thought, *If only I could get a little more 'me time' then I could really focus on improving my personal relationship with God instead of 'doing church' every other day.* That sounds pretty noble, right? No ill intentions there . . . but

I was profoundly misguided. I only came to the realisation after speaking to the first lady of our local assembly, Lady Agnes.

'Lady, I think I need to reconsider how much time I spend in church. I feel like I'm losing out on a personal relationship with God,' I told her in a desperate plea to get her sympathy.

'Son, you know the calling on your life . . .' she retorted.

Like the mother she is to me, she spoke, and spoke, and spoke some more. She reminded me of the significance of serving in church and the impact it had on my personal growth and character development. She also took a detour to briefly draw upon biblical references, share insights from her personal experiences in church, and reinforce the charge given to me to lead the youth and young adults of our church, doing so by example. She probably said a lot more in that two-hour conversation, none of which I can recount—I had already gotten the point after the stern yet loving wake-up call right at the beginning of the conversation. It was in this moment of clarity that I came to the realisation that I had talked myself into walking away from the presence of God, and for fairly 'good' reasons. Nonetheless, it was also in this moment of clarity that I discovered something rather mysterious about the will of God and the role of the enemy thereof—buckle up for this one.

• • •

It's fair to say that many Christians seem to think that once they are in the will of God, everything should line up perfectly. This is false both in theory and practice. Whilst God is working diligently on the plans He has for your life, the adversary is doing the same. I'm usually not one to overemphasize the role of the enemy and give him undue credit but I strongly believe this point is noteworthy.

First, I'd like to define the word 'enemy' which is often synonymous with the name 'Satan'. The original Hebrew term, Satan, is a noun from a verb meaning primarily to obstruct or oppose. Therefore, it is a reference to anything that serves as an obstacle to the workings and ways of God—not necessarily an evil entity personified. From a biblical viewpoint, the word contextually refers to any contrarian who takes up a position or viewpoint that counters the voice of God. Let me give you a prime example found in the Gospels. In this account, Jesus had informed His disciples of the impending betrayal, crucifixion, and death, pointing out thereafter that these things must happen for God's will of redemption to manifest. The dialogue that followed between Jesus and Peter is rather intriguing:

Peter took Him aside and began to rebuke Him, saying, 'God forbid it, Lord! This shall never happen to You.' But He turned and said to Peter, 'Get behind Me, Satan! You are a stumbling block to Me; for you are not setting your mind on God's interests, but man's.' (*Matt 16:22-23*).

This is an OMG moment right here. The other disciples must have thought 'Oh snap, did He just say that?' Allow me to explain why. It was surprising in and of itself that Peter even had the nerve to rebuke Jesus, albeit out of genuine love and attachment to the one he had come to know as his Master. However, Christ's response was even more surprising, considering the fact that He had just declared a few moments before that Peter would be the rock upon which He would build His Church:

'I also say to you that you are Peter, and upon this rock I will build My church; and the gates of Hades will not overpower it (*Matt 16:18*).

Riddle me this: how does one instantly go from being the sanctified builder of Christ's church to being Satan, the rebellious fallen angel that is supposedly responsible for all the world's problems? Frankly, at this point, those that surrounded Jesus must have thought that He was probably bipolar. The answer lies within the fact that the word 'Satan' is not a name—it is a function, an act. It has little to do with personhood and more to do with purpose. Here, Peter was serving the purpose of an obstacle to the plan that The Father had for Jesus. With this understanding, we can now appreciate the reality that some of our problems aren't caused by the devil per se—we are often our own enemy. Sometimes though, the devil himself does creep up on you with an enticing proposition that favours rebellion from God's way and plan.

It's fair to say that many Christians seem to think that once they are in the will of God, everything should line up perfectly.

Let's backtrack to the passage of scripture that we had already begun to examine in Genesis the second chapter. Notice that the chapter ends with Adam and Eve dwelling in Eden—the presence of God—with neither shame nor sin. The insight that may spark your interest here is the following. In the very next verse, which happens to be the third chapter, the serpent appears—from nowhere.

Now the serpent was more crafty than any beast of the field which the LORD God had made. And he said to the woman, 'Indeed, has God said, "You shall not eat from any tree of the garden"?' (*Gen 3:1*).

Now here was a couple who had been put together by God, dwelling in His presence. However, it appears that so was the enemy all along. The point I am trying to make here is this: don't be deluded in thinking that just because you are in God's presence the only voice you will hear is God's voice. That would be utopia. Apparently, utopia has never existed. God was there, but so was the devil. God spoke, and as evidenced by the aforementioned verse, so did the enemy. Just to reiterate this point, let's briefly take a look at the life and ministry of Jesus. The Gospels record a time where Jesus went into the wilderness to fast and pray for forty days and forty nights—He was in the presence of The Father. Yet, the devil was around too:

And after He had fasted forty days and forty nights, He then became hungry. And the tempter came and said to Him, 'If You are the Son of God, command that these stones become bread (*Matt 4:2-3*).

What exactly was the enemy saying to Adam and Eve in the Garden though? Reading further down that chapter, we witness the salesmanship of the devil. The serpent essentially attempts, and with success, to sell Adam and Eve the idea that they could trade the presence of God with something allegedly better—the power of God, carrying the authority to decide what was good and what was evil. The enemy was doing this for two reasons: firstly, he wanted to destroy the relationship between God and mankind. Moreover, he also wanted to destroy the relationship between man and his wife—his intention was to move them from the garden of peace to the boxing ring. But in order to do the latter, he had to do the former. For this reason he sold them an idea that would eventually throw them out of the presence of God. This not only led to an end of their relations with God as they knew it but also led to an end of the way they related between themselves due to the fact that now, unlike times prior, they recognized nakedness and shame:

> Then the eyes of both of them were opened, and they knew that they were naked; and they sewed fig leaves together and made themselves loin coverings (*Gen 3:7*).

What a bummer—they went from being nudists (and loving it), to being ashamed of each other's nakedness and vulnerability. The strength of their relationship had been compromised.

• • •

You see, the enemy was out to derail our relationship and he started by trying to get me to bail out on church. The symbolism here is profound. The aim of the adversary, like in the case of Adam and Eve, was to give me sufficient grounds to leave the garden, the presence of God. But the key thing I missed was this: in order for you to preserve what you acquired in the presence of God, you must remain in the presence of God. The adversary attempts to exchange joy for misery and peace for conflict in every good relationship. He attempts to exchange the garden for the boxing ring. I believe some divorces, certainly not all, could have been avoided if the boxing ring phenomenon was adequately understood. Many couples enter marriage via the agency of the Church, making their vows to each other in the presence of God. After a few relocations, a couple of children, and a number of extra zeroes on their pay cheques, the distance between them and the garden gradually widens. Before you know it, the boxing ring is in full force. I get it—enough with the grim news already. The good news here is this: in every boxing match there is a referee. The role of the referee is to enforce the rules of the game and ensure that neither party is treated unfairly. God plays this role in every relationship, if allowed. For this reason, it remains paramount to keep your relationship centred on Christ.

Believers should not be naïve in thinking that walking in the will of God would necessarily contravene every attack on their relationships; after all, the serpent had access to Eden. In reality, it's the very fact that you walk in God's will and are the recipient of His blessing which attracts the enemy. Without that, he really has no beef with you—you're in the same camp. The key to preserving the relationship is this: remain in the garden. Trust me, the grass is a lot greener on this side of the fence.

Four

Ghana Must Go

Rejection – Refusal – Rebuff

So, as newly engaged couples do, we shared our excitement with family, close friends, co-workers, and a few of our church leaders. For most, it was news that brought elation and complete delight. For a few others, it was a development they had hoped would never happen—the news was welcomed either with indifference or outright disappointment.

Apparently, I was born on the wrong side of the African continent. I should have been born where the flag is green and white, where the land is rich with crude oil. I had only now discovered that I was of an inferior kind and that the borders that separated the nations in our homeland were thicker than ever. It was during this time I learnt that I wasn't good enough for my better half—no pun intended—for she was of the superior kind. Apparently, Ghana was too far from home. Ghana must go.

I remember disembarking Air Arik flight W3064 from Accra to Abuja's Nnamdi Azikiwe Airport in Nigeria. As I walked down the stairs of the aircraft, I looked around trying to acclimatize myself to the new surroundings. It didn't look much different from the place I had just left less than an hour ago. Just then, the lady in front of me turned back with a friendly yet wry smile and asked, 'Are you from Ghana?' in a typical patriotic Nigerian accent.

Quite surprised at the irony of the question, I responded, 'What do you think? You tell me.'

'Well, I think you're from Ghana. You look like one of them.'

I tried not to take offense at that comment as it appeared to be innocent ignorance. I smiled back at her and replied with courteousness, 'Well, I wasn't aware that I looked like "one of them" but yes, I am Ghanaian.'

She smiled.

I smiled back.

I knew that she was Nigerian, not because she looked like 'one of them', but by virtue of the fact that she had the accent and appeared to feel right at home when we arrived.

I couldn't read her well enough, but that encounter just didn't seem right. It was surprising to me that someone who appeared to be studying and living in Ghana could perhaps use such politically incorrect wording when addressing the very people she lived with. Maybe it was a harmless attempt to make conversation, perhaps she was wondering what I was doing in a foreign land. Or could it be that she was hitting on me? I mean, I *was* swaggered out and all that day. But doubt it.

I knew she was Nigerian, not because she looked like 'one of them', but by virtue of the fact that she had the accent and appeared to feel right at home when we arrived.

I was prepared to let that incident go but a couple of other occurrences a few hours later made me realize that the subtle antagonism was a bit more epidemical than previously thought. For instance, the hotel staff constantly glared at me as if to say, 'Hey, you're not from here are you?' What great hospitality for over $150 a night. Later on that day, I recall overhearing two men deliberating on how to transport a few items from one place to another.

'Take it in the Ghana must go bag,' one said.

'Will it fit?' another queried.

'Yes, let's use the Ghana must go.'

Gasp. Insert 'shocked face' emoticon. That was my countenance after hearing that conversation. I mean, I had heard the term used in Ghana in reference to a rather large, multi-coloured striped bag but to hear it used outside my home turf by unfamiliar people was rather discomforting. I liken it to black people who call themselves 'Negro' amongst one another yet take offense immediately when a white person uses the term even in a playful, harmless context. There appeared to be an undertone of Ghanaian mockery instilled in the cultural fabric of the Super Eagles. This derision must have been the source of their acrimony when some heard of Olamide's decision to marry me. Growing up, I knew there was always some sort of *frenemy* between Ghana and Nigeria but I had no idea that the bad blood run that deep. For those of you who are as clueless about the 'Ghana must go' phenomenon as I was, let me take a moment to bring you up to speed with a brief history of these two great nations.

When Ghana gained independence in 1957, many Nigerians migrated to Ghana by virtue of the ruling party's liberal immigration policy fuelled by Dr Kwame Nkrumah's pan-Africanist movement. The relationship became sour when the influx of Nigerians eventually appeared to shift the socioeconomic landscape for indigenous Ghanaians. This led to former Ghanaian President Kofi Busia's Aliens Compliance Order of 1969 which expelled 500,000 Nigerians from Ghana during a three-month period. What Ghana did under this administration would only come back to bite her in 1983.

In the '70s, Nigeria experienced a major oil boom during a time when Ghana was facing a severe drought. Nigeria welcomed Ghanaians into their borders as the need for labour increased. As the oil boom faded in 1983, the people of Nigeria began to blame the Ghanaian immigrants for the prevailing economic woes and frustrating competitiveness in the labour market. This led to the Nigerian government's enactment of the Expulsion Order which ousted 700,000 Ghanaians from the country . . . with their belongings packed up in 'Ghana must go' bags. This episode in history strained relations between the two countries and the love-hate rapport has continued ever since, albeit to a lesser extent today.

• • •

'Are you sure you can marry him? Our cultures are very different,' some said to her out of genuine apprehension. 'I'm not following you to Ghana' others downright disputed, as if to threaten a boycott of any ceremony related to our union. Now don't get me wrong, this antipathy wasn't unilateral. I recall mentioning in passing to one Ghanaian elderly man that I was engaged to a wonderful Nigerian lady. The man's immediate reaction was rather interesting and he went off on a tangent to explain how he had taught his children to marry Ghanaians only. I smiled as I usually do in an attempt to avoid disrespect. In my head I was thinking, *We thank God I'm not one of your children then.*

On several other occasions, some Ghanaians who discovered that I was engaged to a Nigerian often passed snide remarks until they noticed that I was unamused. Such narrow-mindedness confounds me to the point where I begin to wonder if people who call themselves Christians actually seek the will of God in every matter or take comfort in reverting to the status quo. From my experience, it's usually the latter but we will deal with that in due course.

The fact of the matter was this: I had never felt this level of rejection in my life. It was foreign territory to me. It was uncomfortable. I hated it. In times past, I often found that I was either welcomed or celebrated wherever I was. In this case, I was being shunned without a genuine attempt to even get to know me. I often looked back at my life in reflection, reminiscing about the days when a girl I was seeing introduced me to her friends. It felt as though they gazed upon me with proud eyes. I remembered how they passed on their love when they hadn't seen me in a while, how they made time to say hello whenever they were around, how they made me feel as though they had wished more young men were like me . . . how I missed those days.

The fact of the matter was this: I had never felt this level of rejection in my life. It was foreign territory to me.

But here I was, experiencing the phenomenon of 'Ghana must go' all over again. The burden of rejection was intense. I kept it all within without saying a word to my parents, my family, or friends back home. All they knew was that their beloved Jude had proposed to a lady they were very fond of and couldn't wait for the day they would finally tie the knot. The boys were all preparing their best man speeches, the girls were eager to plan a wedding, and the uncles were blocking out time in their busy calendars for the festivities. The events that were to take place in the interim were to be dealt with only by Olamide and I, and boy, was it a heavy burden to carry. Aunty Sola from church, sensing within herself the deep burden, would often stop me in my tracks as I made my way to set up the projector, 'My son, don't feel rejected. God's will shall stand; this too shall pass,' she would say rather matter-of-factly, yet in a soothing encouraging voice.

'Aunty Sho,' as I affectionately called her, 'I know. It is well.'

While these moments always helped a little, I couldn't help but think that this experience was God teaching me a lesson the hard way. That lesson, which has created in me a new-born resilience, is the principle of rejection.

• • •

I mentor a few young adults both inside and outside the
context of church. Although many of them are smart, driven,
and ambitious, they often talk themselves out of applying for
the top jobs and top-tier academic institutions for one reason
and one reason only: the fear of that rejection letter. I remember
the fall of 2009 when I was eagerly applying for internships at
investment banks in London. I knew the firm I really wanted
to work for, but applied to four others for the purpose of safety
and spreading the risk across a diverse portfolio.

The first firm replied.

'We regret . . .'

I closed my email immediately. I couldn't be bothered to
read any word after that.

The second came in.

Rejection.

The third responded.

Rejection.

The fourth firm replied. You guessed it.

Rejection.

At this point, I still hadn't heard back from the firm that
I actually wanted to work for. I flew back to Ghana en route
to the States to continue my third year of university after a
semester abroad in London. At this point, I thought it was
over. *Jude, you'll be spending the summer in Ghana washing your
dad's car,* I thought to myself. Just then I got an email. It was
my choice firm requesting that I attend an interview in London
the following week. Just my luck—wait for me to leave and then
call me back for an interview.

To cut a long story short, they flew me back to London on
an all-expense paid trip for the interview. I got the job. Truly,
there was glory in my rejection.

The truth about humanity is that we long for acceptance. According to Maslow's hierarchy of needs, the third level of human need is interpersonal and involves a sense of belonging. People generally hate to be shunned, neglected, or rejected and the fear of rejection serves as an impediment for many people in achieving their goals and ambitions. This message might not be popular, but I dare say that God uses rejection as a tool to bring glory to His children, and indeed to Himself. Imagine, if I had received an offer letter from any of the 'safety firms', I would have undoubtedly accepted a position at a firm that was only second best. Rejection is necessary and must be readily embraced by all believers.

In our plea to flee rejection, we often forget that Christ was also rejected. They hung the Son of God on the cross not because they accepted him but by virtue of the fact that they rejected His message and teachings. Even on the cross, He was rejected by The Father due to the sin He carried:

About three in the afternoon Jesus cried out in a loud voice, *'Eli, Eli, lema sabachthani?'* (Which means 'My God, my God, why have you forsaken me?' (*Matt 27:46*)).

Why did The Father reject Jesus on the cross? For the sake of our salvation, Christ had to bear our sin on the cross and face judgment by God. The result of which was Jesus being elevated to sit at the right hand of God, and you and I being graced with this wonderful, priceless salvation that we now have. There is glory in rejection:

Fixing our eyes on Jesus, the author and perfecter of faith, *who for the joy set before Him endured the cross*, despising the shame, and has sat down at the right hand of the throne of God (*Heb 12:2*).

As evidenced by the italicized portion, Jesus endured the cross of rejection because He was expecting a greater glory afterward. He didn't fear rejection as He understood the fact that glory was awaiting Him on the other side. Take Joseph as another example, one who was rejected by his brothers and sold into slavery yet rose to become the second most powerful man in the foreign land of Egypt. I am excited to witness the glory that will follow every rejection you have faced and it is my hope that you will share in this enthusiasm with me.

I take comfort in knowing that even before Christ was nailed to the cross, He was rejected by the chief priests and scribes just because of where he came from:

Philip found Nathanael and said to him, 'We have found Him of whom Moses in the Law and also the Prophets wrote— Jesus of Nazareth, the son of Joseph.' 'Nazareth! Can anything good come from there?' Nathanael asked (*John 1:45-46*).

Jesus was immediately written off by virtue of the fact that He was a Nazarene. However, it appears that good things can actually come from Nazareth, and likewise, good things can also come from Ghana. Rejection is only a tool for God's glory to be made manifest in your life. So for the father who walked out on you and your family, there is glory coming your way. For the spouse who rejected you for another person, there is glory coming your way. For the many rejection letters you have received from job and university applications, there is glory coming your way. For every rejection, trust God to receive the glory that comes with it.

There are numerous occasions in my life where I have witnessed this principle at work. I recall the very first day Alphonse gave me the platform to preach at our Christian fellowship on the Bryant campus. It was a struggle but I thought

I did a pretty good job reading the essay sermon verbatim to the congregants. At the end of the sermon, one of my very good friends came to give me feedback.

'What did you think, man?' I asked, hoping to hear a word of encouragement.

'Bro, next time just let Alphonse preach.'

Ouch.

Now, by the grace of God I preach at conferences with many young adults in attendance, and by the leading of the Spirit, many surrender their lives to Christ. It is unwise to despise rejection. Even the Apostle Paul embraced rejection as he ministered the Gospel:

To the weak I became weak, that I might win the weak; I have become all things to all men, so that I may by all means save *some* (*1 Cor 9:22*).

Notice here that Paul says he became *all* things to *all* men, but only that he may save *some*. Why? Because he acknowledged the fact that some people would still reject him anyway. Rejection is a necessary part of life, an unavoidable circumstance. But always remember that God allows it for a reason. He will not leave you to become the reproach of men. For every rejection there is glory.

Nobody can be held accountable for where they were born—that decision lies with God. A man or woman can only be held liable for the character they have. That being said, I am at peace knowing that the principle of rejection works in my favour. I will confidently carry my 'Ghana must go' bag, and do so with my head lifted high. *Selah.*

He will not leave you to become the reproach of men. For every rejection there is glory.

Five

Church at War

Unity – Uniformity – Unison

'Do you see yourself marrying a pastor?' I asked, in a bid to conduct a feasibility study on a long-term relationship.

Pause—brief silence.

I could hear her as she opened her mouth over the phone but I suspected that she was struggling to get any words out.

'Umm, if I'm honest . . . No,' she muttered, as though reluctantly surrendering to a fact she had hoped wasn't the case.

'Ah, I see.'

Pause—brief silence.

'Oh, but my aunts back home always said that I behaved like a pastor's wife,' she said, clearly sensing the need to revitalize hope.

'Ah, I see.'

Pause—brief silence.

I was a little bummed by that. Although I knew within myself that I wasn't necessarily called to be a pastor, I was fully aware of the ministerial calling on my life, in whatever capacity that eventually materialized to be. During the very early stages of our courtship, Olamide and I spent hours sharing our views on God, church, ministry, family, children, and other fundamental values that we deemed to underpin a solid relationship. Needless to say, we spent the bulk of this allotment discussing the Christian Church.

I was a non-denominational Christian. As a child I grew up attending a church that, I would say, had an Anglican slant to their order of worship although unaffiliated with any specific denomination. When I decided to attend church of my own volition rather than by parental guidance, I found myself at one with more of a charismatic bias. As expected, my religious résumé was notably different from hers—she had never been a member of a 'happy clappy' church. The good news here was that, similarly, she wasn't overly fussed about the church one attended but was rather concerned about the fundamental non-negotiable principles that they shared. This, in my humble opinion, is the mark of true character.

But it looked like we were the minority in our viewpoint. Apparently, some denominations were foul, completely unacceptable. It turned out that the church I attended was questionable, had a funny name, and was full of deluded spiritual fanatics. It appeared that believers from one denomination had to avoid others from another, for theirs was the one and only true church. I offer no apologies for my stance on this, I strongly beg to differ and you will soon discover why.

Olamide is an avid blog reader. She spends the lion's share of her recreational time scoping the latest fads on the blogosphere.

It surprises me how she keeps up to date with almost anything and everything—from a story on a newly wedded couple in Lagos as featured on Bella Naija, to the latest tips on how to make healthy dishes on various food blogs. I struggle to take much of an interest as reading for leisure has never been a habit of mine. That was until she shared with me a blog post she had been reading entitled 'Stop Molesting Me With Your Religion'. The author shall remain nameless for obvious reasons.

In this post, the author shared an experience where she was proselytized to by a couple of shop attendants who were attempting to invite her to their church. The shop attendants offered the author a flier and she respectfully declined. To summarize, the evangelizing shop keepers took offense at her rejection (maybe they should have read Chapter Four of this book), and reacted in a manner unbefitting of the faith they professed. In her blog post, the author made very valid points about the ethics and protocol of Christian evangelism that should be adhered to at all cost—people should not be antagonized by one's faith and the shop attendants were wrong in that regard. However, I feel that the author made a few comments that were painfully misguided. There are two points she made that I would like to focus on. The first is that Christians and all religious people for that matter should not 'thrust their religion unsolicited' unto others. Secondly, she signed off on one of her comments saying 'from a Catholic (meaning I am more Christian than you since we were the ones who founded the Christian church)'.

Gasp.

I am all for freedom of speech but that often implies that we get some ignorance thrown in there every once in a while. The interesting thing I found with her blog was that she was publicly berating other Christians for sharing their faith openly, which according to the Book we all deem as our code, is a fundamental principle undergirding the Christian faith. The true reason for her antipathy is revealed in the second point—she felt that she was more of a Christian than the shop attendants because of her specific denomination—not because of her character, her prayer life, or her devotion to God. It was all about her denomination.

I choose to address this in the forum of this book neither to 'spank the author's hand' nor to defame her. I do this because I sense this is a plague that has held the global Church back for centuries. Superficially, we have come to tolerate each other within the Christian faith but in our hearts we still hold a sense of religious aloofness against other legitimate denominations. Unless we admit the truth in that statement, we shall forever remain stagnant—you can forget about a revival. Jesus said it himself, 'Every kingdom divided against itself will be ruined, and every city or household divided against itself will not stand' (see *Matt 12:25*).

I am all for freedom of speech but that often implies that we get some ignorance thrown in there every once in a while.

Not only was the blogger's comment strife inciting, but it was also downright false. Even if the Catholics founded the Christian Church, which by the way is biblically heretical according to the Book of Acts, it still does not make you more of a Christian than anybody. That statement would imply that you are more of a Christian than the Apostle Paul, the Twelve Disciples, and the believers of the Early Church at

Antioch—after all, they were not confirmed Catholics, were they? Being a part of a specific organization neither speaks of your character nor devotion. I remember in high school and college, I signed up as a member of several student bodies but never turned up to a single meeting—it was all for the résumé. Chastising other believers, especially in a public forum, is symptomatic of the fact that Christians can't get their own house in order. How do you invite a guest into your home if he or she can flagrantly see the unkempt state that it is in? These things ought not to be so.

Permit me for one moment to offer some clarity here. I am not placing my stamp of approval on every organization that professes to be of Christ. Jesus said 'you shall know them by their works' when referring to wolves in sheep's clothing. In this chapter, I am defending the legitimate Christian organization, for which purpose I will define as follows: a body that upholds the *full* counsel of the Bible as the only source of divine truth by teaching, preaching, and making disciples of Christ with a true dependence on the Holy Spirit and doing so in love and compassion. This definition is broad and far from exhaustive, but it should weed out some of the organizations that affiliate with Christianity yet do not even remotely resemble the Early Church as depicted in the New Testament.

I have no beef with the existence of denominations. I have a serious grunt, on the other hand, with the mentality of denominationalism. Now, that may sound contradictory but allow me to explain. In my opinion, denominationalism is the mentality that elevates one denomination above another. Denominationalism is the one that says 'I am a Baptist', 'I am a Catholic', 'I am a Pentecostal', and entirely ignores the message of 'I am a Christian—a follower of Christ'. Paul bluntly condemns this mentality in his letter to the Church at Corinth:

Now I mean this, that each one of you is saying, 'I am of Paul', and 'I of Apollos', and 'I of Cephas', and 'I of Christ'. Has Christ been divided? Paul was not crucified for you, was he? Or were you baptized in the name of Paul? (*1 Cor 1:12-13*).

This is what Paul is saying here, translated into today's context: Now I mean this, that each one of you is saying, 'I am Pentecostal', 'I am Methodist', 'I am Catholic', and 'I am of Christ'. Is Christ divided? John Wesley was not crucified for you, was he? Or were you baptized in the name of the Pope?

I believe the problem of denominationalism stems for the nature of the human psyche. The fact of the matter is that people expect everyone to be the same. People tend to equate unity with uniformity—in other words, they subconsciously believe that if we are going to have one purpose and be truly unified, then we must be the same. This is not only impractical but again, biblically inconsistent.

Jesus said 'I and the Father are one' and 'If you have seen me, you have seen the Father'. In Christian theology, we have long accepted the doctrine of the Trinity which acknowledges the Father, the Son, and the Holy Spirit, as members of the Godhead who are individually and corporately the same God. Now, my question here is this: although the Father, Jesus, and the Holy Spirit are one and the same God, are they identical in nature, appearance, and function? Does the Son serve the same purpose as the Father, and the Spirit the same as the Son? A brief study of the scriptures will tell you that the answer here is a resounding 'No'.

Within the Godhead, there is unity and diversity. The Father, Son, and Holy Spirit act as members of the same body operating in unison, but are distinct divine entities that have unique characteristics. If this nature can be found in God, what makes us think that it wouldn't and shouldn't be found in His Church? Are we not meant to be a reflection of God?

• • •

The truth lies in a phenomenon I have coined 'everyone is a different kind of crazy'. As a matter of fact, no one is 'normal'. If God created each man with the amount of effort and precision that the Bible speaks of, it would be a failed attempt if you came out merely 'normal'. Every person created by God came out a little crazy in their own way. I use the term 'crazy' not as a connotation of deficiency but as a mark of uniqueness.

Think about this for one moment: not a single patriarch of the faith recorded in the Bible was the same as the other. Abraham was crazy about believing in the promises of God; David was crazy about seeking the face of God; Solomon was crazy about building edifices for worship (and needless to say, the man was a little crazy about women too); Paul the Apostle was crazy about edifying the church and winning souls for Christ; John the revelator was crazy about the end times—and the list is endless. The supreme purpose underpinning all their 'craziness' was their service to God and the advancement of the Kingdom.

As a matter of fact, no one is 'normal'. If God created each man with the amount of effort and precision that the Bible speaks of, it would be a failed attempt if you came out merely 'normal'.

I believe the same pattern can be seen throughout the various legitimate denominations we find in Christianity—each one is crazy about a particular theme. By my overly simplistic observations, the Catholic Church is crazy about devotion and consecration, the Baptist Church is crazy about baptism (go figure), the Pentecostal Church is crazy about the gifts of the Holy Spirit, the Methodist Church is crazy about salvation and social justice, and so on and so forth. This is not to say that each denomination does not recognize and practice the full counsel of God, but each places an emphasis on one thing over another. Are these things not all biblical? Are they not all working towards the same common goal? Without the apostolic mandate of the Catholic Church where would Christianity be today? How would our social fabric have turned out without the social justice reforms inspired by the Methodist Church? Is it possible that the Christian body could have dwindled without the edification of the Pentecostal Church? The point here is that we are all members of one body serving different functions to achieve the same goal.

Everyone is a different kind of crazy. For instance, I love *Family Guy* but I struggle to get Olamide to watch it with me because she doesn't appreciate the humour like I do. If I'm honest, she thinks I'm 'crazy' for watching such irreligious animation. In her opinion, cartoons should be for children. In the same way, she loves a show called *Don't Tell the Bride*—don't get me started on that. Look around you—everyone is crazy about something and God created them that way. Likewise, within the Church, we are all crazy about God and choose to express our love for God by focusing our efforts on a specific function as part of the greater mandate—to serve God and serve people.

I've witnessed on several occasions members of one denomination shun other denominations with such religious arrogance. It is not unilateral—I have heard Protestants speak of the Catholic Church with condescension and have also witnessed Catholics refer to Protestants in a derogatory manner. I think it's the most unwise thing we can do as a body of believers in one God. We absolutely need each other. If you believe that in your imperfect state, God can use you for His work, why do you deem that another church, in their imperfect state, cannot be used by God? Is it not the same imperfect people that make up a church? I truly believe that each time we demean another denomination we are hurting the Body of Christ. The Apostle Paul tackles this issue at length in the twelfth chapter of 1 Corinthians—I encourage you to read at your own leisure.

Now there are varieties of gifts, but the same Spirit. And there are varieties of ministries, and the same Lord. There are varieties of effects, but the same God who works all things in *all* persons (*1 Cor 12:4-6*).

For the body is not one member, but many. If the foot says, 'Because I am not a hand, I am not a part of the body,' it is not for this reason any the less a part of the body. And if the ear says, 'Because I am not an eye, I am not a part of the body,' it is not for this reason any the less a part of the body. If the whole body were an eye, where would the hearing be? If the whole were hearing, where would the sense of smell be? But now God has placed the members, each one of them, in the body, just as He desired. If they were all one member, where would the body be? But now there are many members, but one body. And the eye cannot say to the hand, 'I have no need of you,' or again the head to the feet, 'I have no need of you' (*1 Cor 12:14-21*).

If you believe that in your imperfect state, God can use you for His work, why do you deem that another church, in their imperfect state, cannot be used by God? Is it not the same imperfect people that make up a church?

I could write about this subject for many more pages but I believe that the point has been made. The human body consists of different parts that do not perform the same function, yet work in unison to achieve the same goal. As the Body of Christ, we cannot expect the hand to look like the leg, nor can we expect the eye to perform the same function as the ear. We have to perform our individual and denominational functions with the primary goal of keeping the body alive and functioning well. The truth is we cannot bring ourselves to agree on every petty issue; frankly, even members within the same denomination do not agree on every single topic. However, one absolute truth we can agree on is that Jesus Christ is Saviour and the world needs Him. Therefore, it's time to stop the bickering and arguing over the pointless grey areas—neither of us is the enemy. The real enemy wants us to spend time arguing on these matters to avoid reaching out to those who desperately need to be shown the love of God.

The key principle here is cultivating the understanding that everyone is a different kind of crazy. My only advice to you is to discover your crazy and serve God diligently once you find it. The blogger's mistake was her religious arrogance which was probably no fault of hers—it is a systemic and endemic problem in the entire Church often preached from many pulpits. Trust me; anyone who hurts the Body of Christ does so at the disapproval of God. The time of war must come to an end. I beseech our Christian thought and faith leaders to call a ceasefire. Let peace, love, and true unity prevail.

The real enemy wants us to spend time arguing on these matters to avoid reaching out to those who desperately need to be shown the love of God.

Six

She Loves Me Not

Agape – Affection – Adoration

I had always believed that I understood the true meaning of love. I mean, I saw love everywhere I turned—from the Danielle Steel books littered around the home to the excessively dramatized romance displayed in our poorly translated *telenovelas* in Ghana. I observed how my sister, Dufie, bawled her eyes out every time she watched *Titanic*. I witnessed how Hollywood movies often depicted a man and woman exchanging affectionate words then ripping their clothes off immediately afterwards. I tried to shut my eyes at this point, especially when my parents were in the room—you know how awkward that moment gets.

I frequently experienced love too. I remember the fuzzy feeling I got inside when my mum surprised me at primary school with a cake on my 8th birthday. I can also never forget the vengeance I felt inside when my sister, Sharon, came home one day with a gash on her forehead—apparently, a bicycle fell on her. I didn't know how that had happened, but at the tender age of five I didn't care. All I wanted to do was walk outside our gate and find someone to shoot my water gun at. I recall how much it meant to me when a girl I cared about told me she loved me and wanted to spend the rest of her life with me. From all the Valentine's Day cards to the sweet text messages, I thought I knew love like no other. It got to a point that one of my high school teachers nicknamed me 'champion lover'. I guess it's pretty obvious why.

The concept of love I had was one that society had taught me. It was the kind of love that was dependent on circumstances, the kind full of passion but devoid of compassion. I am talking about the kind of love that always made me want to be at the receiving end rather than the giving end. We have all been shown this love by pop culture—the kind that hates being vulnerable, the love that always seeks the upper hand in the relationship. This, I discovered, was selfish emotion and was not genuine love.

The concept of love I had was one that society had taught me. It was the kind of love that was dependent on circumstances, the kind full of passion but devoid of compassion.

I remember the first time I said those three magical words to Olamide, her reaction was priceless. I couldn't blame her though, we had only known each other for two weeks. In my defence, I meant those words in a platonic, non-romantic way but there was no way on earth she would have believed that argument.

'I love you,' I said, chuckling in response to a witty comment she had just passed.

I immediately heard the phone drop to the floor and what sounded like a quick scrambling to pick up the pieces of the handset. In utter shock, she must have jolted and lost her grip on her mobile phone.

'Hello? Are you ok?' I asked, wondering if she was all right and whether I had offended her with my words of affection.

Either she was so flattered that I would speak such affectionate words to her or she must have seen me as a complete idiot for pulling that card so early in our courting period. Needless to say, I couldn't help but think that her reaction was an expression of the latter. This conversation temporarily left me with a sour taste in my mouth. I had gone in with confidence and ended the conversation utterly confused. The reaction I received had me questioning my own intentions. Had I been too impulsive? Probably. Should I have waited longer? Maybe. Did I actually mean what I said? You bet I did.

After overcoming the embarrassment from an impaired ego, I had a brief spell of self-enlightenment where I became conscious of how I truly felt towards her. I didn't say 'I love you' because I always had, I said it because I had unreservedly made a choice to love her from that moment onwards. It had become my resolve.

•   •   •

Scripturally speaking, love is a choice that refuses to renege on its commitment. It is a decision made at a specific point in time that abides in perpetuity, turning a blind eye to life's changing circumstances. This is true love, the kind the Bible refers to as Agape.

The LORD appeared to us in the past, saying, 'I have loved you with an *everlasting* love; I have drawn you with unfailing kindness (*Jer 31:3*).

This passage of scripture confounds me every time I ponder on it. If it must be interpreted at face value, it implies that God in eternity past made a decision to love me forever, regardless of my predisposition to Him and irrespective of my future shortcomings, failures, and disappointments. The thing that astounds me more is the fact that as an all-knowing God, it is obvious that He could see the future and predict my every transgression. This suggests that even before I was born, He saw me tell that lie to my parents, and look lustfully upon that girl, and take that item that didn't belong to me, and promote gangsterism through music and lifestyle, yet despite all He saw He stuck by his decision to love me eternally!

Scripturally speaking, love is a choice that refuses to renege on its commitment. It is a decision made at a specific point in time that abides in perpetuity, turning a blind eye to life's changing circumstances.

When a man and woman stand at the altar and make the decision to love each other until death, they are usually going by either the faith or the presumption that their spouse will never change. They vow that they will love each other through thick and thin, but we all know they're desperately hoping that thin will never occur. They promise to love each other in sickness and in health, but are wishfully forecasting a future without sickness. They pledge to hold their love steadfast for richer and for poorer, but prayerfully deny any poverty in their lives. The point I am trying to make is that even when men make that decision to love forever, they do so seeing a forever without problems—a happily ever after. After all, I doubt they would have even made it to the altar in the first place if things didn't seem rosy to begin with. This is the difference between God's love and that of man, that even with His farsightedness of every error and wrongdoing, He still stands by His decision to love unconditionally, even if He does so to His own hurt.

And it *was* to God's own hurt—two thousand years ago.

I have come to the realisation that people don't really understand true love. The Agape kind of love that we learn of in the life of Christ speaks volumes of the sacrifices that must be made in order to validate your love. A man tries to love his woman and pornography at the same time—the two can't be mixed. A woman tries to love her man and a list of checkboxes that represent 'Mr Right' simultaneously—it's not going to work. In order to love something, often times the opposite must be given up in sacrifice. For example, God loves children, so He hates abortion. God loves holiness, therefore He dislikes sin. God wanted companionship with man and as a result He gave up solitude and separateness. And God so loved the world, that He gave up His only begotten Son . . .

For God *so loved* the world, that He *gave* His only begotten Son, that whoever believes in Him shall not perish, but have eternal life (*John 3:16*).

This is the love of God, the kind that compelled Him to give up His own Son. I think humanity would be eternally grateful that I didn't turn out to be God. In all honesty, if that had been the case there would be no redemption for mankind. Imagine giving up your one true possession for the restoration of a people who had not even asked for forgiveness, who despised your act of love, and who rejected the very gift you sent for the sake of peace. I find it more astounding that in the case where man had offended God, it was still God who reached out to man to squash the beef—ironic, isn't it? That is why several new school theologians have come to the conclusion that Christianity is unique, all other religions exhort man to reach up to God and grasp hold of Him through their own efforts. Christianity is the only religion where God reaches down to man.

As much as love is a perpetual decision, love is also an act. Notice that John 3:16 doesn't just say God so loved the world— no one on earth would be comforted by that. The scripture says God so loved the world *that He gave*. There was an immediate action to prove the love that He claimed to have for humanity. And surely, if David could vow that He wouldn't offer a sacrifice unto God that costs him nothing, God was undoubtedly going to outdo David's sacrifice:

2 Samuel 24:24: "No, but I will surely buy it from you for a price, for I will not offer burnt offerings to the LORD my God which cost me nothing." So David bought the threshing floor and the oxen for fifty shekels of silver (*2 Sam 24:24*).

God gave the ultimate sacrifice as a demonstration of His love for you and me. A preacher once said to me, 'You can't outgive God'. Truer words have never been spoken. We live in a world today where no one is willing to cultivate sacrificial love. Husbands and wives are at loggerheads with each other because they are not selfless in their love. Church folk sing to one another 'I love you with the love of the Lord', yet they are rife with envy in their hearts.

I conducted a little experiment with my youth church some time ago whilst I was preaching on this subject. During the sermon, I asked them to open their Bibles to the thirteenth chapter of 1 Corinthians, popularly referred to as the 'Love Chapter' in Christendom. There, I asked them to read from verse 4 to verse 6, as follows:

Love is patient, love is kind. It does not envy, it does not boast, it is not proud. It does not dishonour others, it is not self-seeking, it is not easily angered, it keeps no record of wrongs. Love does not delight in evil but rejoices with the truth. It always protects, always trusts, always hopes, always perseveres (*1 Cor 13:4-6*).

I then went on to share the scripture that says 'God is love' (see *1 John 4:8*) and that by extension, this passage of scripture above can be reworded to have 'God' in place of the word 'love' by simple logical reasoning. I further explained that if that were true, then surely we should also be able to replace the word 'love' with our own names since we were created in the image of God. I asked one member of our youth church to carry out this experiment, replacing the word 'love' with his own name. It sounded something like this:

'Sam is patient, Sam is kind. Sam does not envy, he does not boast and he is not proud. He does not dishonour others, and he is not self-seeking, he is not easily angered, he keeps no record of wrongs. Sam does not delight in evil but rejoices with the truth . . .'

At this point I interjected and comically chided him, saying, 'You realize you're just lying through your teeth right now.'

They all laughed, but they got the point. It was a powerful tool to really open their eyes to the reality that love was not as easy and simplistic as society had presented it to be. The unavoidable truth is that love is always put through an acid test. If you claim to love God, your love for Him will be tested just as His love for you was put to the ultimate test on the cross. What I did not realize when I said those three words to Olamide was that the love I had professed was going to be tried greatly—I probably could have been better prepared for what laid ahead if I had this foresight.

But the prophet definitely had the foresight. I vividly recall when he gave us the prophecy that fateful evening, he said repeatedly in quite a cautionary tone, 'don't let this go, be smart', as if he knew something was going to threaten the foundation of our relationship. Alas, he certainly knew what he was talking about. As alluded to in previous chapters, the fire that Olamide and I came under from various sources and for various reasons was almost tormenting. We occasionally found ourselves wanting to pull the plug on everything. But love always perseveres, it does not give up.

The part I struggled to adopt fully was the patience in love, as naturally, my close friends would testify that I can be quite an impatient person. For an engagement that took a year to gain any material traction, my love was tested to a dimension I had surely never believed was even possible. But through all this, I have found that learning to love the hard way is actually the only way. For God, the price He paid was the life of His Son; for many of us, it will cost us our comfort, our pride, occasionally our dignity, and certainly our most precious asset, our time.

I was fully persuaded that I truly loved Olamide when I skipped an important speaking engagement to watch her run a Race for Life 5k marathon in loving memory of her uncle whom she had lost to cancer. I found it pretty astonishing, in hindsight, that I had started to get worried when I hadn't seen her cross the finish line after what felt like a considerable amount of time. It didn't help that other runners she had started the race with passed the finish line in virtually no time at all, I guess she was just a little slower than I had anticipated. I share this because I find it pretty fascinating how love can transform you into a vulnerable person. Even God, all powerful and almighty, still keeps His guard down with you and me, allowing us to hurt Him with our words, thoughts, and actions. This tells me that being vulnerable isn't a sign of weakness, but one of maturity. It speaks volumes of just how robust the foundation of your love is.

If you claim to love God, your love for Him will be tested just as His love for you was put to the ultimate test on the Cross.

I hate to depict myself as one who is perfect in love. No, I am not a 'champion lover', but one who is continually being perfected in love. It is quite humbling reading 1 Corinthians 13 and realizing that we are all miles away from the target. But, in all truth, we don't reach the target by talking about love; we get there by doing more about the love we profess. Let your act of love speak for itself. Oh, and just for the record, let me set your mind at ease—Olamide totally loves your boy. *Shalom.*

Seven

Pray For Me

Petition – Perseverance – Patience

The period after our engagement was a particularly tough season for us. I don't think I can adequately emphasize how difficult it was to cope. I'm usually a tough nut, my mother taught me how to suffer in silence when it came to my own problems and issues. However, I'm one who cannot bear to see those I care about in physical or emotional pain—it rips me to shreds.

I recall the day I was told the news that my grandmother had passed away. As expected, I was saddened by the tragic report but held it together and kept my game face on. This was until my mother walked out of her bedroom that unforgettable morning before school. As I made my way to the bathroom, she bumped into me halfway down the corridor. I said, 'Good

Morning, Ma,' as I usually do, and made an attempt to walk past her en route to the washroom. She reached out her hand to stop me and with a sweet smile on her face, softly said, 'Papa, I've lost my mum.' She immediately burst into tears. I couldn't even bring myself to comfort her. Failing to get any words out of my mouth, I immediately rushed to the bathroom, sat on the floor, and wept until I was all cried out. I couldn't stand to see her so dismayed and it certainly gave me no respite that my hands were virtually tied. I couldn't bring granny back.

During our engagement season, I felt like it was history repeating itself. I knew that we were both under the same pressure and stress but I couldn't stand to see her carry the weight of that burden. It eventually got to a point where I was willing to walk away just to preserve her sanity.

'Olamide, I love you too much to let you go through this. If it would give you back your peace of mind, let's end things here with our sanity intact.'

'Jude,' she said sternly, 'that doesn't make me feel better.'

'So what do you want me to do, sweetheart? I hate seeing you upset.' I retorted. She looked up at me teary-eyed and muttered, 'Pray for me, please. I need you to pray for me.' I looked into her eyes and smiled, thinking to myself how profound her words were.

'Okay, I will do.'

I was so moved by her appeal for prayer that I purposely decided to carve some time out of my day just to pray for her on a regular basis. But if I learnt anything during my university days under the tutelage of Alphonse, it was that people ought not to pray amiss. The members of our campus fellowship prayed together daily using scriptures to direct and reinforce our prayer points. The purpose behind this was to ensure that

whatever request was made to God was done so in accordance
with His will, His ways, and His works.

'So what do you want me to do, sweetheart? I hate
seeing you upset.' I retorted. She looked up at me
teary-eyed and muttered, 'Pray for me, please. I need
you to pray for me.'

It is amazing how foolish some prayers we lift up sound
when tested against the Word of God. I remember when I was
in high school, years before I became a Christian, I used to pray
in ignorance that God would help me commit a misdeed; and
then when things went pear-shaped, I'd pray again asking Him
to bail me out. I was constantly firefighting. As you can see, I
really took the principle of 'ask and you shall receive' to heart
during Sunday school—clearly that's all I paid attention to. It
wasn't until I accepted the Lord that I realized that all those
prayers were diabolic.

It wasn't God I was praying to all along. On the contrary, I
was wishing on my personal genie, but this genie came without
a bottle for easy access. I thought I could just wake up and pray
for anything and that if I shut my eyes hard enough I'd be heard
and my request would be granted. Clearly, my misguidance
knew no boundaries but I certainly wasn't the only one who
believed they could get away with this sort of prayer life.

To be honest, anyone remotely affiliated with the Christian
faith believes that prayer is important to a certain extent. Owen
Carr's famous quote, 'A day without prayer is a boast against
God', is widely shared in Christian circles. Martin Luther
notably said 'To be a Christian without prayer is no more

possible than to be alive without breathing'. People generally understand the significance of prayer, but few truly know and appreciate the principles guiding it. The fervent effectual prayer that avails much is that which is aligned to the perfect will of God. But how does one align their prayers to the will of God? It's simple . . . by reading the Word of God.

Over the past few years, I have observed that almost everyone wants to go to Heaven but very few of them want to see God when they get there. In the same way, many believers love to tell God their mind, but only a handful want to know the mind of God for their lives. They have retired the Bible as an antiquated piece of literature with no modern-day relevance. I can't blame them. I used to think the same thing until I started using it as the basis of my prayers.

It wasn't God I was praying to all along. On the contrary, I was wishing on my personal genie—but this genie came without a bottle for easy access.

In all honesty, some of the requests we make to God are answered not on the basis of God's perfect will for our lives, but His permissive will. There is a stark difference between the two. In layman's terms, the perfect will of God is what He wants for you and the permissive will of God is what He permits you to have by virtue of your adamancy. In the parable of The Prodigal Son, Jesus speaks of the relationship between a father and his two sons, likening that to the relationship between God and man. In this anecdote, the younger son prematurely asks his father for his share of the inheritance. The knucklehead then squanders all his inherited wealth in riotous living in a foreign land. After an extended period of poverty, he returns to daddy broke and a hot mess. The father warmly embraces his prodigal younger son and throws him a block party, as a subtle way of saying 'you never should have left; my perfect will all along was for you to be here'.

The interesting thing here is that the boy's father actually gave him his share of the estate and permitted him to leave the house in search of a foreign land. This tells me that although God knows what is best for you, He does not impose His will on you. The onus is on you to allow Him to carry out His perfect will in your life. And sometimes, that perfect will may not necessarily be the most comfortable path . . .

And He withdrew from them about a stone's throw, and He knelt down and began to pray, saying, 'Father, if You are willing, remove this cup from Me; yet not My will, but Yours be done' (*Luke 22:41-42*).

I am intrigued by Jesus' petition at the point in which He realized the imminence of the cross. He essentially prayed, 'God, if you would permit, please take this burden from me. Nonetheless, let your perfect will be done'. In other words, if Christ had His own way He would not have been scourged and crucified, yet He believed that the perfect will of the Father needed to take pre-eminence over His personal will. And the perfect will of the Father implied a death so powerful that its reverberations can still be experienced today.

The perfect will of God is what He wants for you, and the permissive will of God is what He permits you to have by virtue of your adamancy.

This is why it is critical to pray for the will of God to be done in every aspect of your life. But doing so requires regular reading of the Word of God in order to ascertain God's mind concerning a particular situation. If prayer is a way for man to communicate to God, how does God communicate back to man? Do we serve a God made out of wood and stone? Does our God not have a mouth that He can speak? Often times, the answer to many of our prayers can be found right in our Bible.

'And you will *know the truth*, and the truth will make you free' (*John 8:32*).

I love this verse—it's been the one-stop shop for all the answers to my prayers. In search of financial freedom, career freedom, marital freedom, and what have you, the answer to that pursuit can be found in the truth. But the caveat here is you must know that specific truth. Jesus tells his disciples here that they can find solace in the truth, but it has to be the truth that they know. In other words, if you are sick and are praying for healing yet do not believe that God is a healer, you cannot be set free of sickness by that truth. If you are imploring God for a financial blessing but do not know that God is a provider of every good thing, you cannot be set free of poverty by that truth. It is the truth you know that will set you free. And how do you know the truth? You guessed it, by reading the Word of God.

The same is true for the principle of faith. The Bible stipulates that it is pointless to pray without faith because your request will not amount to much.

And without faith it is impossible to please Him, for he who comes to God must believe that He is and that He is a rewarder of those who seek Him (*Heb 11:6*).

But how do we get faith?

So then faith cometh by hearing, and hearing by the word of God (*Rom 10:17*).

Need I say more? The inter-relatedness of prayer, the will of God, faith, and the Bible cannot be substituted by any other strategy. In order to pray effectively, you need to have faith and this can only be acquired by studying the Word of God. The knowledge acquired also grants the person praying the ability to plead their case according to God's perfect will, being guided by His mind concerning that particular matter.

• • •

I realized that I had to pray that the perfect will of God would be done in her life, and more broadly, in our relationship—that whatever God had started with us, He would bring to a perfect completion. It appeared that the more we prayed on this, the more things seemed to remain at a stalemate. The silence during this impasse was more deafening than ever. It didn't look like anything was changing for the better, if at all. It got to a point where I felt it was time to stop pestering God on the same matter over and over again. What I hadn't discovered was that God's apparent silence on the request was intentional all along—He was waiting for the appointed time:

There is an appointed time for everything. And there is a time for every event under heaven . . . a time to tear apart and a time to sew together; a *time to be silent* and a *time to speak*. He has made everything appropriate in its time (*Eccles 3:1, 7, 11*).

God chooses when to 'answer' our prayers according to His calendar, not ours. An example of this was when Jesus was informed of the ailing Lazarus who was virtually staring death in the face. Jesus intentionally attended to other issues and was later told that Lazarus had died. The natural mind would be justified in questioning Jesus as to why He did not respond with the urgency that the situation apparently called for. But Jesus had said 'This sickness is not to end in death, but for the glory of God, so that the Son of God may be glorified by it' (see *John 11:4*).

In the end, Christ raised Lazarus from the dead. It is evident from this account that God occasionally uses silence and perceived delay as a tool to bring glory to Himself. How would God have shown His power of resurrection had Lazarus not died? It may feel like God is unmoved by your plight or unresponsive to your requests, but be convinced that He will answer at the appropriate time. But in all this, you should remain persistent in prayer—don't stop knocking on that door.

In the Gospel according to Luke, Jesus is recorded telling a parable of a persistent widow seeking justice from an unrighteous judge who did not fear God nor respect man. The judge was initially unwilling to grant her justice but eventually threw in the towel because the widow kept bothering him for legal protection. This is where it gets interesting:

And the Lord said, 'Hear what the unrighteous judge said; now, will not God bring about justice for His elect who *cry to Him day and night,* and *will He delay long* over them?' (*Luke 18:6-7*)

The principle is simple: those who travail persistently in prayer grab the attention of God and consequently get an answer. As evidenced above, God will not delay in answering their requests, He is always on time. Neither Olamide nor I had ever prayed in our entire lives as much as we did during this period. I do feel, with the benefit of hindsight, that it was another way God used to amplify our dependence on Him.

Prayer is you telling God, 'I need You, I can't do this alone.'
And boy does that turn heads in Heaven.

It is my hope that Christians would embrace the sort of
prayer which is guided by the Word of God. Bear in mind,
however, that just because God did not fulfil your request
doesn't mean that your prayer was not answered. It has been
answered all right, with a resounding 'No'. God knows what's
best for us and sometimes the requests we make to Him can
be disastrous if He honoured them. Jean Ingelow, an English
poet and novelist in the eighteenth century, put it best when
he said 'I have lived to thank God that all my prayers have not
been answered'. In this same spirit, Richard Needham was once
quoted saying 'God punishes us mildly by ignoring our prayers
and severely by answering them'. Let's admit it, sometimes our
prayers can be completely out of line with the mind of God for
our lives.

Bear in mind, however, that just because God did
not fulfil your request doesn't mean that your prayer
was not answered. It has been answered all right,
with a resounding 'No'.

But what remains a surety is that prayer moves the hand
that moves the world. And you needn't worry about eloquence
or verbosity in speech. God can even make sense of a confused
prayer. Some time ago, I had a few friends over to lounge and
share a meal. I then asked one of them to pray over the food
before we ate. One young gentleman then stood up, closed his
eyes and said 'Lord, with this food, let your will be done'. It
was the most inappropriate time but the rest of us burst into

laughter. We had absolutely no idea what that prayer meant but, in hilarity, responded with an 'Amen' all the same.

The thing here is God still understood and appreciated that prayer. He knows your request even before you ask and is more concerned about the earnestness of your heart than your elocution. Pray without ceasing, and the God who answers prayer will surely hear you and come to your aid.

Eight

Reflections

Benediction – Beatitudes – Benison

As I reflect on the events of these past two years, I am thankful for every struggle, pain, and trial that Olamide and I have faced, being fully convinced that our union is genuine and resilient. Growing up loosely exposed to Nollywood drama I could have sworn these things only happened in movies—little did I know that it was a reflection of real life experiences, and worse, that I was next in line.

To be honest, I would have preferred that things panned out a different way. If I had taken the pen from God's hand to write my own story, it would have read very differently to the one portrayed in this book. I would have chosen a love story with no pauses, a narrative that flowed from beginning to end with no hiccups.

I would have kept the tension associated with the fear of the unknown to a minimum. I would have been single for two years after my previous relationship. The ideal sequence of events would have been to meet someone within my late twenties, have a three-year relationship, and finally settle down in my early thirties. Yes, I would have loved the peace of mind that came along with taking a Ghana passport holder to meet the family. It would have been a perfect courtship, perfect engagement, and a not-so-perfect marriage but who cares, no one would read that part of the story anyway. I would have gotten away with the greatest façade ever, but at least it would have been an enjoyable fairy tale.

I would have chosen a love story with no pauses, a narrative that flowed from beginning to end with no hiccups.

Yeah right—I don't care much for pretence. I thank God that He held on tight to that pen. And truthfully, I'm glad that I chose the less travelled road—I now see why that is the case. As if the fear of the unknown wasn't distressing enough, people always made it a point to make their small talk about the wedding that we hadn't, as yet, set a date for.

'How was your weekend, Jude?'

'It was great, thanks.' I would reply, hoping that the small talk would end there. It never did.

'So, how are the wedding plans coming along? Set a date yet? Are you excited?'

'Dude. No. And if you ask me again I'll throw a wet fish at you' . . . is what I wanted to say. But seeing as Aunty Nana Ama raised me well, I often responded with 'Not yet, but I should have an update for you soon. I'll keep you posted.'

• • •

It definitely hasn't been a fun-filled journey but I have come to the realisation that it was a necessary one. The time spent in the wine press was critical in developing maturity and character, two traits that are seldom achieved by any other means—they are products of time and experience. Warren Buffet echoed this principle when he said 'No matter how great the talent or efforts, some things just take time. You can't produce a baby in one month by getting nine women pregnant'.

I frequently wondered why we had to plough through so many hurdles for such an extended period of time. I only now recognize the essential life lessons they have taught me.

The first lesson is painfully simple but worth mentioning due to its criticality in life: no matter what you do, people will always talk. I found myself watching a Nollywood movie the other day entitled *Mr. Ibu*. For a film rampant with comical theatrics, the director surprisingly managed to communicate, and with some seriousness, the importance of taking people's opinions with a grain of salt.

A father and his son were seated on a bicycle riding together on a journey from their home in rural Nigeria. Upon seeing this, one bystander deemed it fit to share his unsolicited opinion free of charge: 'How can two people use one bicycle at the same time?' he criticized. In response, the son dismounted the bike and trekked alongside as his father pedalled. Further on, another concerned citizen reprimanded the father, labelling him as a wicked and selfish man for riding whilst he watched his son follow along on foot. In response to this reproof, the father and son exchanged places. A passer-by then came along to share her views on the new situation, chiding the son for his countercultural act of disrespect for elders. Out of frustration, the father and his son decided to give up on riding the bike all together—it appeared that it wasn't going to be worth the headache. As luck would have it, another onlooker further down their journey mocked them saying, 'how foolish both of you are to walk when you clearly have a bicycle at your disposal'.

Sigh—you just can't win with men. Don't even try it. I quote myself in *Crossroads* when I say that people are psychologically inconsistent beings whereby an act applauded one day could very well be condemned the next. The opinions of men, if all adhered to, would leave you utterly confused if not entirely ruined.

I remember when I was first toying with the idea of a relationship with Olamide months prior to actually hearing the prophetic affirmation. I shared the prospect of what appeared to be a likely pursuit to a closed group of family and friends. I find it astonishing that some who initially were, at best, agnostic about the relationship have now become one of its greatest proponents. This is not to shame anyone, far from it. It is perfectly understandable why one's early inclination would be to maintain the status quo—inertia is a basic human nature. Nevertheless, I am thankful for my stubbornness in this regard. If I sense that I have not heard from God myself, I hardly ever go by anyone's opinion on a matter.

The opinions of men, if all adhered to, would leave you utterly confused if not entirely ruined.

I would have made one of the greatest mistakes of my life if I had sought to please others rather than fulfil my purpose. This is not to suggest that one should be recalcitrant and unyielding to direction. By all means, actively seek guidance, prayer, and a second opinion. But it should be just that—a *second* opinion. Over the years, there has developed a spiritual dearth wherein believers make the opinions of their pastors and leaders their own without consulting the scriptures for themselves. They blindly adopt strange doctrine without conducting due diligence at the first instance. They use the will of their parents as a proxy for the will of God. They are led by feelings and reactions rather than a genuine sense of purpose. Don't become like the father and son duo whose actions were imprudently driven by the opinions of men. Seek the voice of God in everything you do and you will surely make your way prosperous.

The second lesson I want to leave as a takeaway is this: things will not always go according to your preconceived design, but they will definitely go according to God's plan, if permitted. As I mentioned before, I wanted things to pan out a certain way even after the prophecy was given. If indeed God was behind this relationship, why couldn't everything be picture perfect? Every now and again, I would think to myself, *God, you've given me a huge mandate but I don't seem to be in a situation that befits the call for marriage.* I was a relatively young man who had recently started a career as a banker. I didn't have much to my name. Although some viewed me as a mature person who had accomplished a reasonable amount for his age, I certainly understood why others raised the aforementioned points as issues of concern. Truthfully, I wanted to be in a certain place before I ever put a ring on it. But apparently, God works in mysterious ways. You see, it's not about where you find yourself; it's about what God is calling you to do.

While they were there, the days were *completed* for her to give birth. And she gave birth to her firstborn son; and she wrapped Him in cloths, and laid Him in a manger, *because* there was no room for them in the inn (*Luke 2:6-7*).

I find the mandate of the Virgin Mary rather interesting in this context. In the second chapter of the Gospel according to Luke, we learn of the birth of the Saviour of the world, Jesus. In the preceding chapter, we are told that an angel of the Lord appeared to Mary and informed her of the impending pregnancy. What believers easily recall is the fact that Mary gave birth to Jesus in a manger. But what they easily overlook is the subtle detail that she did so *because* there was no room for her in the inn. This implies that she tried her best to get into the inn and resorted to the manger after an unsuccessful attempt. The maternity ward she actually wanted was the comfy inn. I can't say I blame her.

Put yourself in Mary's shoes for a moment. You have just been told that you are the lucky one to give birth to the immaculate Son of God—no pressure. Of course, given such an honourable mandate, you would love nothing more than to bring this child into the world in grand style. And then all of a sudden, you learn that you cannot give birth in the inn you had hoped for and would have to settle for a manger. It's a pretty tough pill to swallow. It's like expecting to ride out to your wedding in a Rolls Royce, only to walk outside the hotel and find that a Picanto awaits your royal highness.

The thing that I admire most about Mary is the fact that she didn't let the situation deter her. Yes, she had expectations of bringing forth the Saviour in style and comfort. When she realized that the inn was off bounds, she didn't let that stop her from giving birth. She understood that it wasn't the environment she was giving birth in that mattered; it was who she was giving birth to. The calling was far greater than the circumstance. The thing to note here is that God uses contradictions like this to bring glory to Himself. He wanted to prove to humanity that He could turn the least noble of births into the most memorable of deaths.

Through this revelation, I realized that it wasn't about the situation I found myself in. Rather, it was about the purpose of my calling, one that I had to answer regardless of whether or not conditions appeared favourable to the naked eye. I just had to get it done. Therefore, my question to you is what are you waiting for? We both know that God has called you to do something, yet you are patiently waiting for the inn. Quite frankly, the door of that inn isn't going to open to you. Give birth right there in the manger and watch God's glory unfold in your life.

She understood that it wasn't the environment she was giving birth in that mattered; it was who she was giving birth to. The calling was far greater than the circumstance.

By virtue of these experiences, I have quickly dismissed the naïveté I had about people. Olamide always said that I was excessively optimistic and saw the best in others, even when there was a glaring reason to doubt their intentions. The truth is, she was right. And that hasn't changed. What has changed is my deceitful notion that I have never had, do not have, and will never have enemies. I thought I was immune to people disliking me. I mean, I'm a pretty charming guy if I may say so myself. I believed that if ever I offended anyone for any reason, it was because that individual probably misunderstood me. I assumed that I could have no enemies and that people did things with my good in mind.

Right, that was until I came back to earth.

A painful reality of life is that people do not need a reason to dislike you, and they certainly don't need an ulterior motive to be against your cause. I have had people call me all sorts of names without even having a conversation with me before. Some have passed distasteful remarks about me for writing a book at my age—'after all, what does he know?' It's a sign of pride to believe that no one can dislike you. Even God has enemies and He is quintessentially perfect—by definition, He has never committed a wrong. It actually doesn't make any sense if all men favour you; it says something about your character if that's the case.

'Woe to you when all men speak well of you . . .' (Luke 6:26)

The painful reality of life is that people don't need a reason to dislike you, and they certainly don't need an ulterior motive to be against your cause.

If all men spoke well of you, it tells the world that you haven't taken a stand on anything. It speaks volumes of your double-mindedness and the fact that you simply cannot be trusted. Take a moment to examine the public lives of all the greats: which one of them hasn't once been criticized? Even Jesus Christ, the Son of God, was maimed for apparently no reason. Pilate conceded that He couldn't find a single fault with Him, yet they still hated Him to the point of death. But understand one thing: God will always speak for you when people are prejudicially against you.

To subvert a man in his cause, the Lord approveth not (*Lam 3:36*).

• • •

As I ponder upon the past few years, I have really prayed for a forbearing heart to forgive those who have knowingly and unknowingly offended me. It's easy to tell others to forgive and forget until you have to place your feet in those enormous shoes. Forgiveness, however, is not a forgotten memory; it is a memory without revenge.

As I look to the next stage of my life and marriage, it is my prayer that posterity will judge me kindly. I can only hope that the life I have lived thus far is worthy for my children to look up to. As one who is stubbornly reticent about my personal life, it surprises me how much I have shared with the world in the hope that someway, somehow, someone will be enlightened and encouraged to achieve more.

But if you've learnt nothing at all by reading this book, I'm sure you've still come to some sort of conclusion about Scotland. Indeed, good things do happen in Glasgow. However, to my future children, this story has nothing to do with Glasgow at all.

Kids, I have just told you an incredible story. This is the story of how I met your mother.

Acknowledgements

Appreciation – Applause – Admiration

I cannot acknowledge this incredible woman without first paying tribute to the God that she so diligently serves. I remain eternally grateful to God for the transformative work He did in her life several decades ago. All who have known her have been blessed in one way or another. Mum, you are the backbone of our family and more, personally, that of my character and success. Although you may never wear a clerical collar, Heaven bears record of the priestly mantle you carry in the eyes of all who have been blessed by an interaction with you. I add my voice to that of your husband and children to celebrate you whilst you're still on this side of Heaven.

Dad, for a high-ranking naval officer you are one of the most gentle and kind-hearted people I have met during my time here on earth. I am indebted to you for your selfless love, support, and willingness to lend an ear to every concern and issue I have brought to you for guidance. I am grateful for the wisdom you shed abroad when I brought to your attention my desire to get married. It is obvious that you are the quintessential father, steward, and custodian of the children to whom God has entrusted.

Few have left a lasting impression on me like this couple have—Bishop Dick Essandoh and his wife, Lady Agnes Essandoh. To leave your names off this letter of appreciation would be an injustice to the principle of honour. You have been outstanding mentors to both Olamide and I. As such, I humbly dedicate this book to you. For your patience, thoughtfulness, and constant encouragement, I owe you a debt which I can only hope to repay in kind during my lifetime.

For the sheer rarity of her kind on earth, I have no choice but to acknowledge the woman I hope to make my bride one day, my beloved Olamide. It's rather ironic that you have remained by my side in sickness and in health, through highs and lows, and all this without making any binding vows at the altar. I have found in you a love and character like no other and for that, I had to put a ring on it (Beyoncé, I took your advice). I bless the day our paths crossed.

To all who have played an instrumental role in our relationship, I would like to express my sincere gratitude to you:

Samuel and Charlene, I am forever grateful to you both for the introduction—I'll gladly take it from here. Thank you.

Lady Gifty, Minister Mac, and the Young Adults of ACI London, you have been an incredible support system. I wish I could name each of you individually but I am certain you know yourselves. You guys are amazing—may God truly reward you.

Aunty Sola, what a source of encouragement you have been to me, thank you. I am especially grateful for your sound relationship advice and your education on Nigerian culture. Whenever doubt creeps in, you are the one who always knocks some sense back into me. I owe much to you.

I'd like to take this moment to specially acknowledge my future parents-in-law, Mr and Mrs Awosemo. I know that it hasn't been an easy decision giving your daughter away to a young man you hardly know, particularly one with no legal ties to the land you call home. I recognize the many times I may have erred in oblivion to cultural protocols and traditions and I am thankful for your understanding. Through it all, I have come to appreciate and admire the importance you both place on family. I am truly grateful to God for your lives, raising a gem like Olamide is undeniably reflective of the quality of parental guidance she received from you. Thank you both for being awesome.

• • •

And now to the shout-outs: a big thank you to my wonderful siblings who have been incredibly supportive and encouraging these past few years—people can only dream of being blessed with family like you. Aunty Naana and family, you always know how to revive hope in me, thank you for being there. Mabel, the words in this book would not have been transcribed without your God-inspired direction—I'm thankful for your life. To all my close male and female friends, I truly appreciate your friendship. The amount of support I receive from you is overwhelming and I honestly could not have asked for better friends.

Special thanks to my publishing team: Nana Dufie Addo, Alphonse Asare, Gerald Kusi, Mariolla Baffour, Yanfo Hackman, Adobea Atuah, Frempomaa Duah, Arama Ribeiro-Thompson, Mabelline Appiah, Naa Akwetey, Richie Donkor, Raquel Larnyoh, and Rodney Appiah. I really couldn't have done this without your help—I am forever thankful.

Finally, to all *Crossroads* enthusiasts, thank you, you make the ministry truly worthwhile.

God bless you.

For Discussion

❖ 'I decided to stay single for the next few years and maybe consider marriage at some point in my mid-thirties—to a Ghanaian.' What do you think drove the author to this point?

❖ 'I knew there was always some sort of *frenemy* between Ghana and Nigeria but I had no idea that the bad blood run that deep.' In your experience, is this true? How would you describe the relationship between Ghanaians and Nigerians?

❖ Do you feel that the author's assessment of the state of the Church is fair? What do you think about the state of the Church globally?

❖ How would you describe the author's attitude to adversity and offence? Do you believe that some situations could have been handled better?

❖ 'It's fair to say that many Christians seem to think that once they are in the will of God, everything should line up perfectly.' Are you guilty of this?

❖ 'Love is a choice that refuses to renege on its commitment. It is a decision made at a specific point in time that abides in perpetuity, turning a blind eye to life's changing circumstances.' How true is this statement? Is the author's understanding of love scriptural?

❖ 'People are psychologically inconsistent beings whereby an act applauded one day could very well be condemned the next.' Have you experienced this before? How do you treat the opinions of people?

❖ 'It wasn't God I was praying to all along. On the contrary, I was wishing on my personal genie—but this genie came without a bottle for easy access.' How reflective is this of your prayer life? What's your opinion on how to pray to God?

❖ What does this book teach us about purpose, patience, and perseverance? How are these three things linked?

❖ 'A painful reality of life is that people do not need a reason to dislike you, and they certainly don't need an ulterior motive to be against your cause.' How does the author feel about prejudice? Do you agree with this statement?

❖ 'As one who is stubbornly reticent about my personal life, it surprises me how much I have shared with the world in the hope that someway, somehow, someone will be enlightened and encouraged to achieve more.' How has this book inspired you? What changes do you plan to make going forward?

Suggested Further Reading

Going All The Way: Preparing for a
Marriage That Goes the Distance
by Craig Groeschel

I, Isaac, Take Thee, Rebekah: Moving
from Romance to Lasting Love
by Ravi Zacharias

When God Writes Your Love Story: The Ultimate
Approach to Guy/Girl Relationships
by Eric & Leslie Ludy

The Five Love Languages: The Secret to Love that Lasts
by Gary D Chapman

I Kissed Dating Goodbye: A New Attitude
Toward Relationships and Romance
by Joshua Harris

Other Books by the Author

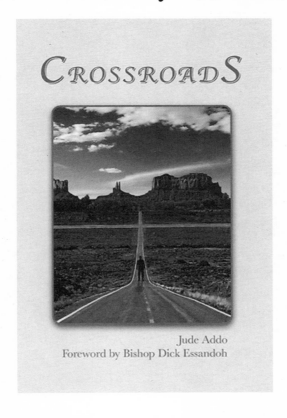

Crossroads tells the exhilarating story of a young man's spiritual journey from the vantage point of secular events that transpired in his life. Intellectually stimulating in content and autobiographical in format, this book promises to inspire the reader to strive for both an intimate relationship with God and excellence in secular pursuits.